Inside stories

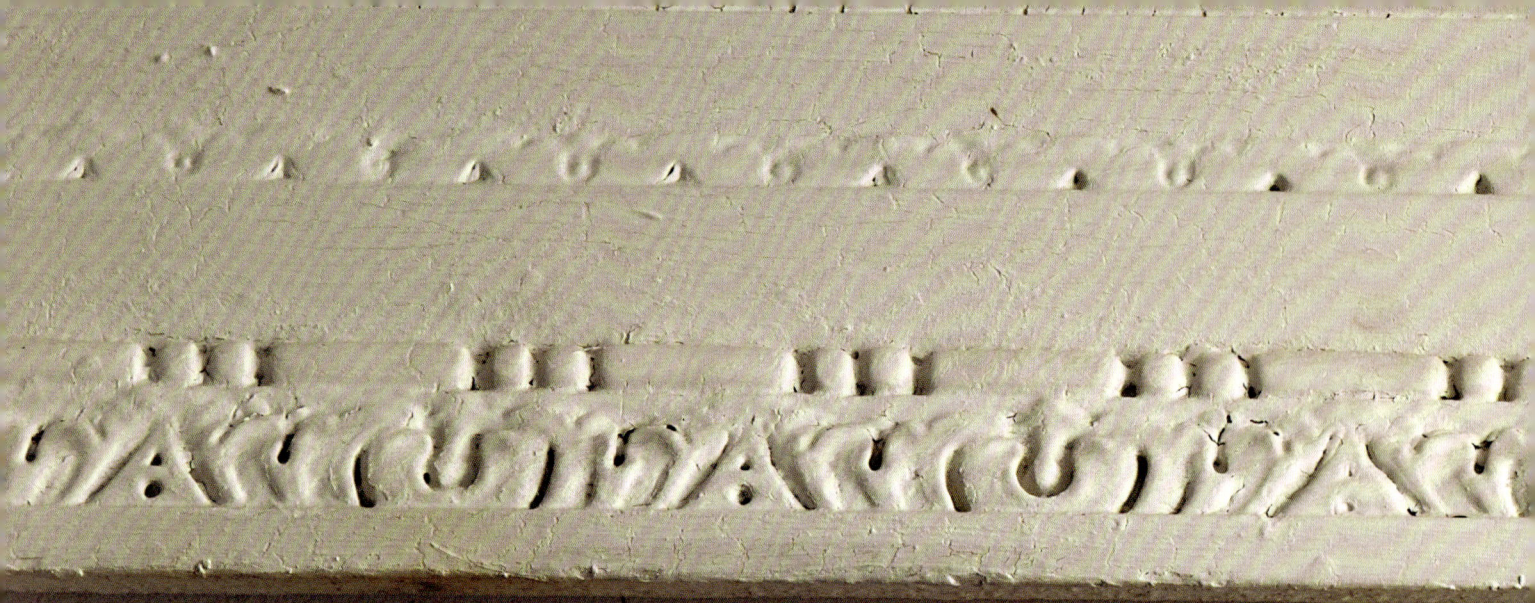

Inside stories

CURATING AND DISPLAYING THE STUFF OF LIFE

HILARY ROBERTSON

with photography by
ANNA WILLIAMS

RYLAND PETERS & SMALL

First published in 2014. This revised edition published in 2025 by Ryland Peters & Small 20–21 Jockey's Fields London WC1R 4BW and 1452 Davis Bugg Road Warrenton, NC 27589 www.rylandpeters.com email: euregulations@ rylandpeters.com

10 9 8 7 6 5 4 3 2 1

ISBN: 978-1-78879-700-9

Printed and bound in China

A CIP record for this book is available from the British Library. US Library of Congress Cataloging-in-Publication Data has been applied for.

The authorised representative in the EEA is Authorised Rep Compliance Ltd., Ground Floor, 71 Lower Baggot Street, Dublin. D02 P593, Ireland www.arccompliance.com

FSC
www.fsc.org

MIX
Paper | Supporting responsible forestry
FSC® C008047

Senior Designer Megan Smith
Commissioning Editor Annabel Morgan
Location Research Jess Walton
Head of Production Patricia Harrington
Art Director Leslie Harrington

Styling Hilary Robertson
Photography Anna Williams
Additional Photography Claire Richardson
Additional Text Kathleen Hackett

contents

introduction

My preoccupation with interiors started early. From the age of four, I had access to a wild natural playground at the local village school that comprised a big field of coarse grass on the edge of ancient woodland. We were allowed to roam freely under the supervision of a couple of cosy matrons who patrolled the grounds. For the most part, our imaginary games were based on home-making. Along with an ad hoc 'family' of friends, I made camps; alfresco homes with rooms defined by twig walls. There were leaf beds, acorn cups in the kitchen, leaf curtains, daisy-chain decorations, tree-bark rugs. Time stood still while I swept the earth floors with my holly branch broom or arranged my imaginary children's leaf pillows on their mossy beds.

This early domesticity did not translate into an adult love of housework, but my passion for the aesthetic part of nest-making flourished, first in my teenage bedroom and then within the grey cinder-block walls of a tiny university room on campus; the blank canvas for a De Stijl-themed primary colour scheme inspired by a Rietveld chair (an 18th birthday present made for me by my godfather). It seemed to me that in a chaotic and uncertain world, it was therapeutic to create one's own 'private Idaho' and have control over it, however humble, small or poorly funded it might be. As long as I could make some pleasing arrangement of twigs and branches or rip pages from *Casa Vogue*, plaster walls with postcards from museums and stack pebbles like a novice Andy Goldsworthy, I might feel 'at home', and my library of preferred visual references would never fail to nourish me.

I hardly knew what a stylist was or did when I left university, but the moment I understood what styling involved, I knew that I must try to be one. Hunting, gathering, arranging and rearranging; styling was my default setting. As a grown-up, I have had the chance to make quite a few homes, many (if not most) of them with a very limited budget. I'm a fan of limitations; infinite possibility can be scary and being able to spend a lot on an interior does not guarantee the beauty of the result.

When my son was ten days old, we moved into a house we had spent a few months tearing apart. It wasn't the most practical home for new parents with a tiny baby: a pretty but narrow Victorian house with three floors that was more suited to a family with teenagers who could separate themselves on the top floor or hide out in the little cricket pavilion in the terraced garden outside. I was new to motherhood, so my decorating decisions were based on pre-baby concepts for stylish living: gloss white-painted floorboards (labour-intensive, slippery and hard), pale linen sofa (impractical), silk taffeta curtains (an invitation to sticky little hands). I longed for a bungalow with wall-to-wall carpets. But just as we fixed the last few details, my husband was offered a job in New York. Off we went.

As I am as fond of the journey as I am of arriving somewhere new, my three-year-old and I took the Old World option and sailed to New York on the Queen Mary. I took six enormous suitcases, leaving most of my lovingly collected things (and most of our furniture) behind in storage or farmed out to friends. I can't pretend that it wasn't painful to part with the stuff I had amassed over the years in the excellent junk shops, markets, car boot sales and antiques centres of Hastings, London and just about anywhere else I ever visited. I tried to convince myself that living without my stuff would be salutary; a sort of cleanse. Perhaps I could even reinvent myself as a minimalist? The universe snorted 'fat chance!'

I started out in NYC thinking that I could be another person. Perhaps I didn't want to be a stylist any more? I decided that, in my Englishwoman Abroad incarnation, I should try on a new persona. We were living in a very practical apartment that we had sublet from a family who were trying out living in the country in upstate New York. At first, it was rather liberating to try someone else's lifestyle, but it soon became disorientating. We were supposed to be there for a year, but their experiment didn't work out, so soon enough we had to move to another sublet, in which we struggled to feel at home. Eventually, when the owners of the second sublet had to take away their furniture and ship it to their new home in San Francisco, we went to Brimfield Flea Market in Massachusetts, a trip that reignited my relationship with 'stuff'. New old stuff. Hurrah!

It was inevitable. For me, making a home really was about the layers of things that are acquired over time; things that have stories and remind you of places and people and a feeling of discovery. It's also a way of showing the world who you are: the museum of me; a key to your personality. I think that all 'stuff', even the most quotidian, can be beautiful if it is arranged as if it is important. And Beauty (whatever Beauty is to you) is balm for the soul.

NATURE TABLE

This heavy stone table is my stage set for many still lifes. I can't move the table, but I change it constantly, especially when I have been to the flower market and have some extraordinary flowers or seasonal branches to find a home for. It's a good exercise, as it forces me to play with collections. Here, I assembled pieces of lab ware, mixing science with nature (this page). The following week, this evolved into a garden table, where a 'Dinner Plate' dahlia adds a delicious dollop of carmine to the scene, a shade that is picked up in the pinkish tinge of the succulents (opposite).

how to arrange your stuff

intuitive
SEEMINGLY RANDOM ARRANGEMENTS

seemingly random

IMAGINE THAT YOUR COMPOSITION IS A PAINTING AND GIVE IT A CLEAR STRUCTURE, THEN INCLUDE SUBVERSIVE, LIGHT-HEARTED OR DISPOSABLE ELEMENTS.

If you want to learn how to display objects with the skill of a professional stylist, a good way to start is by examining every artistic arrangement you encounter with a critical eye. Looking at Dutch still-life paintings or Irving Penn photographs can teach you more or less everything you need to know about subject matter, scale and how to group things. Close observation will also reveal that the negative spaces, the spaces in between your chosen objects, are as vital to the whole composition as the objects themselves.

It doesn't surprise me that the painter Giorgio Morandi spent years moving a collection of vessels around his studio until he saw an arrangement that he wanted to capture on canvas. I could happily do the same with the stuff that I collect without getting bored. Creating something beautiful is compelling and addictive. It's meditation of sorts and, I suspect, just as good for the soul. You don't need anything except for your eye, your chosen objects and an idea of what you would like to achieve in an aesthetic sense. Even if nothing else in your room pleases you, you can transform one surface to your own satisfaction.

When you are engaged in setting up a still life, there will always be another way to do things, another possible configuration, but it is up to you to decide when the composition is finished. Sometimes the greatest satisfaction comes from dismantling a composition; probably because that's when it starts to feel less contrived. 'Set it up, then mess it up' seems to be the stylist's mantra.

Before I had any money to spend on buying objects for my home, I found them – on a beach, in a park, on a street. My first collections were an extension of the school nature table: driftwood, bird's nests, fossils and feathers. And gathering things together on a windowsill in my urban flat was my way of escaping to another place, a reminder of the possibilities that existed outside my immediate surroundings. I couldn't always manage to be in the place that I longed for, but I could evoke the sense of it.

Any arrangement of objects, however simple, provides visual clues about the preoccupations and motivations of the person who made it. This explains why houses without any personal bits and pieces on show often seem rather soulless and disappointing to the viewer, why magazines must sometimes hire stylists to make 'perfect' homes look more lived in. The aim is to suggest, as artfully as possible, that normal everyday things go on in rooms that otherwise seem unnaturally pristine.

Most arrangements evolve without a plan and will change as time passes – that's all part of their charm. But there are guidelines that will help to produce a pleasing result. The 'tablescape' – a term invented by renowned English decorator David Hicks – combines things that are both useful and decorative; you decide on the balance between the two. When it comes to putting it together, the key is to vary shape and scale, grouping together items of a similar size. On a low table, a pile of hefty books juxtaposed with a tray corralling smaller things like keys, letters, stamps, matches and a vase of flowers or branches can make a graphic patchwork resembling a landscape viewed from above.

For a console table, think of reproducing the Manhattan skyline with its contrasting layers, reflecting the tensions between different materials and styles of architecture. Or imagine that your composition is a painting and give it structure: a foreground, a middle ground and a background. The inclusion of subversive, light-hearted or disposable elements – a child's drawing or family photos – will prevent any arrangement from appearing too self-conscious.

GOING DUTCH
Dutch still lifes are always in my mind as reference points for displays. In this Belgian kitchen (opposite), two simple vessels, a black jug and a grey vase, sit on the worksurface with an enamel mixing bowl and some wooden boards (which are used as plates in this household). The arrangement captures the moment of preparation before setting a breakfast table and shows how even the most utilitarian objects have a quiet beauty.

PERFECT PROPORTIONS

Josephine Ekström's home in Sweden is pared down, almost minimal and the colour scheme is monochrome. However, she is a master of compelling still lifes, which add drama to the space. Josephine often uses a picture to ground an arrangement. In this case, Deborah Bowness's wallpaper panel with a photographic image of a 1960s chair serves as the backdrop for a large Asian ceramic pot, a plaster jaguar and a contemporary balloon-shaped table lamp on a low wooden table. Instead of placing books on top of the table, they are sculpted into two graduating towers underneath.

BUILDING BLOCKS

When I'm searching for props, I'm always attracted to strong sculptural or geometric shapes that I might include in a composition. The sensual brass shape in the bottom right-hand corner of the picture above is a bookend, one of a pair by Ben Seibel (1918–1985), a prolific American industrial designer whose work has become very collectable. Seibel's pieces, both practical and highly decorative, help to add structure to bookshelves. Similarly, the vintage wooden shape with a hole in the middle and the brass square cages bring a masculine edge to this 'tablescape', the term invented by decorator David Hicks for his method of arranging all manner of smaller things on side tables, consoles, bedside tables or coffee tables. By clustering things in groups determined by colour, shape or material, such as the repeated circular motif seen left, he created harmonious arrangements that were more than the sum of their parts. Think of all the small things – boxes, figures, trinkets – that are scattered about a room brought together in a tableau.

SHELF LIFE

In Leida Nassir-Pour's bedroom (opposite), a single shelf runs alongside her bed bearing a selection of thought-provoking objects that reflect Leida's taste for Victorian and Edwardian style; an alligator doctor's bag, apothecary bottles, a glove mould, two jay birds perching on a branch and a papier mâché bust conjure a scene from a Gothic novel.

TIGHT SPOT

The roofline slopes towards this tiny window in a French barn bathroom (below), leaving an awkwardly shaped space that decorator Annie Moore has filled with two galvanized metal buckets holding dried branches. Their muted colours and textures echo the roughly plastered walls and unfinished woodwork perfectly.

UNDER GLASS

Opposite her desk, traveller and collector Alina Preciado keeps an industrial table set with an ever-changing exhibition of precious pieces, each enclosed by a glass cloche. An elaborately embroidered silk Mongolian child's boot, an incense holder and decorative brass vials of kohl eyeliner from India are each singled out as things to appreciate, conjuring memories of journeys taken or suggesting ideas for future ones.

narrative

ARRANGEMENTS THAT TELL A STORY

personal altars

CHILDREN PLAY LIKE THIS ALL THE TIME, SETTING UP UNLIKELY NARRATIVES
INVOLVING DINOSAURS AND FARM ANIMALS, ROBOTS AND BRICKS.

The act of choosing an object and displaying it immediately invests it with significance, however ordinary it might seem. In my living room, I brought together a miniature boat, two anchors, two chunks of brain coral and a plaster spoon mould. The ghostly white galleon – a kite with a bamboo skeleton – was too ethereal, too beautiful to fly in the park and then just fold away. Instead, it leans at an angle on a console table, grouped with some chalky flotsam and jetsam that seemed to complement it, conjuring up an imaginary scene from a sea shanty.

Children play like this all the time, setting up unlikely narratives involving dinosaurs and farm animals, robots and bricks. The charm of such arrangements is often enhanced by disparity of scale and the incongruity of the elements assembled. Every time I move around my cache of objects, I try to let something unpremeditated happen, as if drawing a picture with my eyes closed – letting what the Surrealists called *hasard objectif* play its part.

If I analyse the pattern of my collecting over the years, the themes are clear. The sea and everything associated with it – shells, coral, boats, fish, pebbles – are the totems of my favourite escape from the quotidian grind of the city. But of course, I am not alone in my attachment to nautical and coastal items, and to souvenirs of seaside holidays. Mementoes of seaside holidays or foreign travel are peddled in abundance in resorts all over the world, in souvenir shops clustered along promenades and boardwalks. The fact that so many of us want to acquire an Eiffel Tower paperweight, a postcard or a bundle of Provençal lavender shows how much human beings desire to be surrounded by things that transport them to another place, time or moment. We hold on to a particular stone or shell not only because it is a tactile object but also because, just as taste and scent evoke powerful Proustian memories and feelings, it connects us to the past.

If someone who had never met you came to your home when you were absent, what would he or she discover? Would your possessions tell your story? Could the vistor decode you?

The process of photographing people's homes for magazine features can reveal much about their personalities and predilections, occasionally leaving an indelible impression. A visit to Barbara Hepworth's studio in St Ives, Cornwall, has always remained in my mind; although the sculptor had been dead for many years, the space was still alive with her thoughts and unfinished work. Such is the power sometimes contained in inanimate objects. Although I have never used them (or at least, not yet), I collect paintbrushes, potter's tools and old encrusted paint palettes because I relish the idea of what they can do and have done, and they fuel a fantasy of having my own studio one day.

Things that are well used, worn, torn, faded or rusty fascinate me more than the pristine and box-fresh. But I can also appreciate the minimalist's imperative to find one astonishing object so perfect in material, concept and execution that it can stand alone on a table to be admired, a tribute to its owner's skill in acquisition as well as the skill and talent of its creator.

THE CHICKEN OR THE EGG?
Stephen Johnson's tiny three-room apartment is decorated around a few idiosyncratic themes and colours; spheres, the colour blue combined with hits of red, nautical ephemera and an Escheresque geometric pattern all recur. Even in this corner of the kitchen (opposite), he mixes whimsical decorative stuff with kitchenwares. A framed picture of an egg cup by Martyn Thompson torn from a magazine, a white ceramic chicken by Astier de Villatte, a concrete mushroom, a red, blue and white patterned cup again by Astier de Villatte and a disembodied hand holding a bowling ball all add characteristic quirkiness to the practical space.

NATURE MORTE

For photo shoots, I usually have to buy what my husband refers to as 'shoot fruit': real fruit that my family is forbidden to eat until the job is over. These wax or rock crystal grapes and eggs made from marble and onyx will never decay, and are fun to work into still lifes instead of the real thing.

EXPERIMENTAL ART

In a corner of her living room, a painted screen depicting a science laboratory sets the scene for Liza Sherman's collection of lab ware set up as an imaginary experiment on a metal chest of drawers (opposite left).

ON DISPLAY

Liza Sherman travelled widely before putting down roots in New York. The console table in her living room (above) is a vehicle for a still life of objects trawled from many far-flung journeys: a silk kimono from Korea, vintage artist's palettes and beaded headpieces from Africa. A Dogon ladder leans against the right-hand wall.

FLOWER GIRL

The still life on top of this black-painted armoire gives many clues to the preoccupations of its creator, Lindsey Taylor. A landscape gardener and florist, Taylor's tiny two-room penthouse apartment is calm and white-painted, almost minimalist, but its plainness is offset by vignettes where she combines her twin obsessions: flora and fauna and handmade ceramics. The monochrome colour scheme is a foil for the pale, subtle shades of dried branches and flowers.

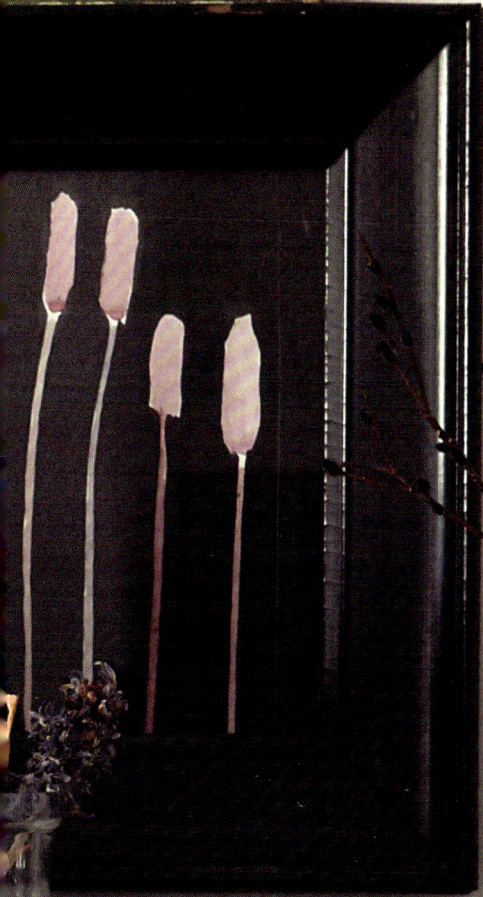

practical
THE DISPLAY OF USEFUL THINGS

divide & rule

Sometimes objects have a tendency to clog up our homes, lurking ungracefully in all the wrong places and creating an unsightly jumble. My entrance hall, for example, should be renamed the dumping ground. Against the advice of every book on feng shui ever published, its contents reveal to visitors the worst of my family's habits: unopened mail, shoes, broken umbrellas, a (now invisible) sculptural coat stand that is toppling over under the weight of many seasons' overcoats.

But every now and again, I come across a home where the inhabitants have found ways to arrange and sort even the most mundane stuff in an inspiring way. These homes force me to reconsider my dumping ground and remind me of the need for greater discipline. The display of practical things demands a process of ruthless editing and categorizing that an eclectic collector like me finds rather suffocating. But how I envy those open shelves full of copper pots and pans, handmade ceramics and vintage silver cutlery/flatware in French jam jars! To assuage this envy, I have made a deal with myself to acquire more things that are both beautiful and useful. In an ideal world, everything that I use in my kitchen will be a tactile, hand-crafted object of beauty: olive wood chopping boards from Tuscany, curvaceous ladles carved by the artisan hipsters of Portland, Oregon, blown glass instead of mass-produced moulded glass, goose-feather dusters from Sweden, hand-loomed linens from Latvia… it's a slow process.

Once you possess the lovely things (even some basic Duralex glasses or plain white porcelain plates look great en masse), be guided by the principle of divide and rule. Simply store or display objects in groups with identical or related objects, and keep the groups distinct from each other. I've never been fond of those operating-theatre kitchens with sleek 'units' hiding everything from view, and the effective control of clutter doesn't mean having to conceal everything. In a kitchen, for example, keeping implements to hand on a shelf or storing cooking pans in wooden crates seems eminently sensible. Outside, why not arrange tools and pots on a potting table or wooden shelf, as Jocie Sinauer does in her courtyard garden? I will admit to an obsession with

baskets and a hankering for hooks to suspend them from. In a hallway, a collection of market baskets can be useful for the storage of items such as shoes, gloves, scarves and dog leads. One day, I hope to be the sort of person who has a large selection of straw hats hanging on a wall – an installation that suggests that you are an expert gardener, a global explorer, a bee-keeper, a garden-party regular, and generous enough to keep hats for the use of guests as well. I feel exactly the same way about a boot collection.

When it comes to storage, don't underestimate the potential of an ordinary wooden ladder or a more elegant, tapering, apple-picker's ladder. A ladder leaning against a wall in a bathroom makes an excellent substitute for a towel rail. In a kitchen, equipped with butcher's hooks, the ladder makes a space-saving vertical storage device for pots, pans and utensils. I've also seen a ladder installed horizontally like a pot rack above a work station in a kitchen, with the *batterie de cuisine* dangling from it.

Some of the best storage pieces I have discovered were originally designed for the display of merchandise in shops. Among these are two vintage mannequins that now adorn my home. One is laden with an ever-increasing collection of necklaces, rosaries, beads and chains, while the other wears whichever coat or jacket I'm most fond of at the time.

ALL FOR ONE
In her New York apartment, Sydney Maag corrals an eclectic selection of porcelain, glided glass tumblers, a basket filled to the brim with matchbooks from NYC restaurants, vases, tureens, bonbon dishes and her son's pottery on a tall painted shelf unit standing against a blackboard-painted wall in her kitchen. Trays hold different sorts of vessel, with one brass tray containing the bottles of spirits that comprise her cocktail cabinet.

OPEN SEASON

Landscape designer Lindsey Taylor's studio apartment is fitted with a floor-to-ceiling wall of storage that's essential in so small a space. Open alcoves allow her to display pieces from an ever-growing collection of ceramics, together with shells, feathers and flowers; flora and fauna found on walks.

CORNERED

Interior designer Bea Mombaers has arranged her kitchen, which is part of a combined living area, so that plates, bowls, cutlery/flatware and utensils are kept on hand on open shelves rather than in cabinets (above left).

WOOD WORKS

A clutch of wooden spoons, a stack of hand-turned Early American bowls and a hanging chopping board are kept next to the range in this kitchen in upstate New York (above).

INSIDE OUT

Antiques aficionado Jocie Sinauer treats her courtyard garden as a room to be furnished in the same way as an interior room. A tall, sturdy shelf unit serves as a place to store empty terracotta garden pots, the smallest ones contained in wooden trays (above left).

HANG IT ALL

A shallow balcony in Copenhagen is just big enough for a folding table (above). Metal plant troughs filled with plants hung from the railings save space.

PLATFORM

Josephine Ekström makes an instant garden by raising up a selection of potted plants on a low concrete bench (opposite). She varies the height of her arrangement by sitting a fig on an upturned wooden crate. On the ground, a fruit crate holds more miniature topiaries.

curatorial

A CABINET OF CURIOSITIES

curiosities & collections

VINTAGE, SALVAGED AND RECYCLED OBJECTS ARE JUST AS ACCESSIBLE
AS NEW ONES, WHEN YOU KNOW WHERE TO FIND THEM

There is a fine line between collecting and hoarding. When I met my husband, he had three storage spaces packed with everything from rare Dutch bicycles to Scandinavian art glass. Naturally, he could explain his motivation for holding on to every single item – one of the bicycles, for example, was to be flocked and hung on the wall as a sculpture.

I was an amateur by comparison – a vague, unfocused *flâneur*, a dilettante magpie to his calculating collector. I was certainly addicted to flea markets, junk shops, antiques centres and car boot sales, but it hadn't occurred to me to approach these retail outlets with a strategic plan. He educated me in how to build up a collection through clever acquisition, and together we devised plots for buying trips.

From the moment we started trawling markets together, he has been my *aide de camp*, my negotiator, my second pair of eyes. So much so that trying to buy anything in an ordinary shop is almost impossible when you are with him, since he has a horror of new things. In fact, the word 'new' is the biggest insult he can muster, as it denotes a sort of laziness that he despises. Why buy mass-produced objects when you can find something that was made in good-quality materials at a time before the invention of flat-packed particle board and injection-moulded plastic? I am all in favour of the democratization of design, but my personal preference is for a combination of old and new. Vintage, salvaged and recycled objects are just as accessible as new ones when you know where to find them, and there is the added bonus that they might increase in value one day.

Once you identify something that you are attracted to, you may want to keep going and acquire many other iterations of the same thing – and that is how a collection builds up. When my husband and I moved to New York City, we discovered things that we hadn't seen in Europe, such as the Civil War shaving mirrors that he avidly began to collect and the mid-century Ben Seibel bookends resembling Henry Moore sculptures that I discovered on my first sortie to the enormous flea market at Brimfield, Massachusetts. Of course, just about anything can form the basis of a collection. Feathers, shells, stones and autumn leaves look wonderful in box frames with labels that record the date, time and place of finding – and natural things also have the advantage of being free. Artist Stephen Antonson gathered up all the lost single gloves he found on the winter streets of Brooklyn. Then he matched each one up with a partner and framed them for a Valentine's Day exhibition. The paper messages from fortune cookies could inspire the same treatment.

When you decide to create a new collection, the more esoteric your ideas, the better. Humble workmen's tools are easy to come by but look extraordinary when hung in groups on a wall, as in the studio of sculptor Constantin Brancusi. If you are more attracted to a particular colour or material than to a special type of object, you could assemble a cabinet of curiosities containing everything from bird skulls to coral.

It's all very well being a wily hunter-gatherer but, unless you want to become a dealer, it is essential to integrate your acquisitions into your home somehow, and this means acquiring some structural pieces that can house and enhance growing collections. I love wooden apple crates, which can be stacked, hung in a row and lined up vertically or horizontally. When you have many things of different sizes in a collection, you can show them off strikingly by arranging them into groups according to size before putting them on display in separate compartments. By isolating distinctive pieces, you can appreciate them anew and enhance their perceived value. Open armoires, small wall cabinets with glass doors or without doors, printer's trays for tiny collections – all make excellent containers.

SOAP OPERA
The impact of some collections is often determined by how easily they can be displayed; a piece of furniture that complements the objects is required. In a bathroom, this painted wooden dresser with glazed doors is ideal for the eccentric assortment of soaps crowding its shelves (opposite).

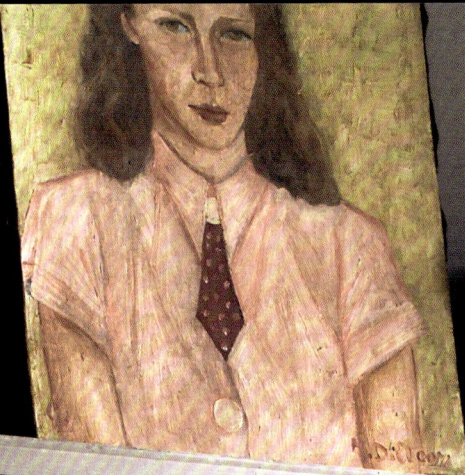

HATS OFF

This minimalist bedroom (opposite left) establishes its ethnic theme with two elements: the textile hung above the bed on the chimney breast, and the extraordinary montage of headgear that's symmetrically mounted in both alcoves.

AFTER MORANDI

These curiously shaped mottled enamel kettles circa 1910 are grouped in a still life that pays homage to artist Giorgio Morandi, master of the tertiary colour palette (above). His still lifes of vessels have inspired countless imitators, and there is something both meditative and obsessive about these arrangements.

WHITE ON WHITE

Annie and Colin Moore like to visit their local
flea market in the South of France with a plan
and a small budget. Defunct electronic goods
(literally white goods) – a Casio keyboard, a black-
and-white television and an analogue telephone
– are combined with a top hat, a tea service,
vellum boxes, piles of interiors magazines, bird's
nests and a pigeon for a charming tableau of mostly
useless things in their barn's white sitting room.

COLOUR BLINDNESS

In my black dining room, I have assembled all sorts of white objects on a marble-topped side table on one side of the chimney breast (this page). Above the table hangs a collection of Civil War shaving mirrors and a steer's skull. The console table opposite displays some sculptural white chalk chocolate moulds that can be balanced in many configurations.

IN THE FRAME

Jocie Sinauer combines a collection of small mirrors hung 'salon' style with additional empty silver-gilded frames propped against the wall (below). Similar in tone are the natural things – coral, pebbles, driftwood and a turtle shell – laid on the table.

FLORAL TRIBUTE

Annie Moore bought an antique portfolio of pressed flowers and covered a whole bedroom wall with them (opposite). The sinuous organic shapes modernized by frameless glass suit the updated rustic vibe of the room.

stories
told
by
real
homes

neatnik

DEFINITION: SKILLED AT
EDITING, NEATNIKS AIM TO
LIVE SIMPLY AND EFFICIENTLY,
SURROUNDING THEMSELVES
WITH JUST A FEW WELL-
CHOSEN PIECES.

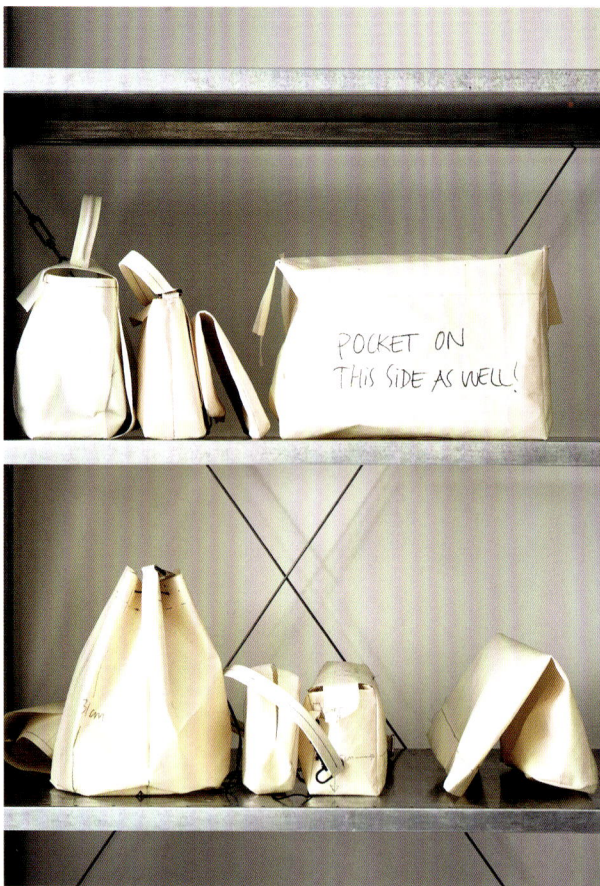

Handwritten note on bag: POCKET ON THIS SIDE AS WELL!

Yvonne Koné

When is a neatnik not a neatnik? It may seem contrary to include the neatnik in a book about 'stuff'. I am not, and will never be, a neatnik. I wish I could be, but my love of collecting precludes me joining that particular decorating tribe. As a stylist, I have developed a certain ruthlessness when it comes to editing my own possessions, but I'm always impressed by the way that a bona fide minimalist is able to sort the wheat from the chaff, especially when they can simultaneously make their spaces feel warm and personal – welcoming, even.

Imposing a limited colour scheme is an effective approach to creating a calmer, more cohesive space. Having fewer things, or only keeping hold of things that you really love, is another. Freed from the burden of clutter, neatniks are apt to exude a preternatural sort of calm. They have stuff, but are not slaves to their stuff. They know where to find things and tend to be very practical when they design an interior.

Before you throw everything out, consider this: living with less requires rooms to have 'good bones': elegant proportions, beautiful light, sharper architectural detail. Yvonne Koné's apartment in Copenhagen has exactly the right bones for her rigorous approach to decorating: a uniform black, grey and white scheme that extends throughout all the rooms. The floors are the perfect bleached/limed oak, the walls are matt white throughout, the windows are bare. They look good undressed because the 19th-century vernacular architecture of her building features large windows with deep sills and interesting catches (no ugly double glazing). Yvonne's floors are mostly bare too, except for a couple of textile runners. Of course, they are exactly the right shade of pale that bounces the soft Scandinavian light around, flattering every plane with its hazy, soft focus.

It's hard to believe that three children live in this haven of order and tranquillity. What's more, accessory designer Yvonne, who recently started her own line, has opted to work from home in a modest room equipped only with a long table, a sewing machine and a wall of utilitarian metal shelves, stacked high with boxes of buckles, studs, leather swatches and handbag and shoe samples in black (mostly) nubuck.

The only decorative touches that make the edit are the framed art, much of it illustrations by Yvonne's husband (who illustrates children's books), and some sculptural 'found' lighting. A wall of built-in floor-to-ceiling shelves between the living area and the office is the catch-all for potential clutter; it contains books, records and a few select 'objects',

PAPER BAGS
Yvonne's handbag samples, stored on metal shelves in the home office, are made of canvas before they are fashioned in leather (above left).

PARED DOWN
The low bed in the bare-bones master bedroom eliminates the need for bedside tables (opposite). Walls are left plain, and the only colour in the scheme comes from an ethnic rug.

FREED FROM THE BURDEN OF CLUTTER, NEATNIKS ARE
APT TO EXUDE A PRETERNATURAL SORT OF CALM. THEY
HAVE STUFF, BUT ARE NOT SLAVES TO THEIR STUFF.

QUICK CHANGE

A modular sofa means that Yvonne can change the look of her living area (this page) very easily. Two wooden pallets serving as a coffee table are just the right height for the low seating, and they too can be separated and rearranged in an instant. There are no curtains, throws or cushions to clutter the zen space. A vintage industrial lighting fixture adds a sculptural shape. The simple teapot, mugs and shallow bowl also contribute to the calm of the space (opposite).

such as the oversized gilded finials that Yvonne found on eBay and her collection of depictions of African hairstyles.

The low-slung grey sofa is modular and can be reconfigured in several ways, but at the moment it is arranged either side of two low wooden pallets repurposed as coffee tables. A sculptural potted fig tree punctuates the scene with its height, colour and shapely leaves – one organic element in the monochrome room.

There is a monastically simple bedroom at the centre of the layout with a low platform bed flanked by two reading lights, a black armoire and a red-painted vintage table that's a judicious jolt of colour. But that's it – no other visual distractions. For sensuality, Yvonne is more likely to indulge in lighting one of the many scented candles that are dotted around the place than scattering cushions.

The kitchen–dining room is tucked away at the back of the apartment. Here, the plain white cabinets are free of handles, the vintage ply and tubular metal chairs were salvaged from a school and some darkly glazed handmade ceramics are the only pieces kept to hand on open shelves. The room is as plain and pure as a Shaker's; simple, functional and handsome.

YVONNE'S RIGOROUS APPROACH TO DECORATING – A UNIFORM BLACK,
GREY AND WHITE SCHEME – EXTENDS THROUGHOUT ALL THE ROOMS.

SELF-CONTAINED

Yvonne's 15-year-old daughter has a scrupulously organized study area in her bedroom, where stationery supplies are contained in a series of boxes, and pencils stand up neatly in Perspex containers (above left and right). Under the long, slim desk, Yvonne has tucked a small chest of drawers, which is used for extra storage. The S-shaped hooks on the small clothes rail (left) are a clever way to hang tote bags, belts and scarves.

CATCH-ALL

Stretching all the way across one wall, the bespoke storage unit (opposite) contains all Yvonne's potential clutter. It is the most colourful and graphic spot in the apartment. Against the cool white walls, book spines appear as multicoloured stripes.

THE KITCHEN IS AS PLAIN AND PURE AS A SHAKER'S: SIMPLE, FUNCTIONAL, HANDSOME. BARE WINDOWS FLOOD THE ROOM WITH LIGHT FROM TWO ASPECTS.

ONLY NATURAL

Utilitarian tubular steel and plywood chairs are teamed with a narrow dining table in the kitchen–dining room (opposite left). Yvonne accessorizes minimally, with one variety of flower in a curvaceous and fluted white vase, and fruit in a shallow ceramic bowl.

IN MONOCHROME

White walls and white kitchen units, topped with a black counter, run along two walls of the kitchen (above). Yvonne keeps the bare essentials that she uses everyday close to hand: a Bialetti coffee pot, a teapot and spices in glass jars on open wooden shelves and a stack of soapstone plates on the windowsill.

Annie
Moore

Camellas Lloret has one of those fortress-like
facades that reveals nothing of the charm that
lies within its massive 18th-century stone walls.
Accessed via a narrow winding lane in a sleepy
hilltop town outside Carcassonne, its gargantuan
double doors open not into the gloomy entrance
hall you might expect but onto a peaceful
courtyard garden that's all neat green box,
trickling water and crunchy pea gravel.

Serial renovators Annie and Colin Moore have made this
latest project into a rambling *maison d'hôte* without resorting
to any of the familiar French decorating clichés. After several
renovations in France, Annie has developed her own style of
neatnik comfort; bedrooms are furnished with simple wooden
beds topped with sturdy, wool futons and painted in darkly
sophisticated grape-grey or green-grey, or any variation on
that theme. But she is not averse to a smattering of pattern
and has preserved panels of rather 'granny' wallpaper,
choosing to paint her preferred sober shades around them
and somehow succeeding in transforming retro beige florals
into something quite modern and chic.

In previous interiors projects, Annie had resisted anything
as decorative as these papers, but since the building had so
many original features — marble fireplaces, cornices,
panelling and so on — she decided to experiment with wall-to-
wall pattern, swathing the dining room in a snaking oak-leaf
design that even covers the rectangular wall lights designed
by Colin. The leafy motif in this room echoes the way Annie
approached the orangery, where the scented leaves of potted
geraniums make organic patterns on the chalky white walls.
Windows throughout are dressed with panels of floaty linen
hanging from narrow wrought-iron poles, tiled floors are
strewn with cowhides and piles of classic white-covered
French paperback novels fill the bookcases.

FRENCH ACCENTS

The bones of this part of Annie's rambling French home are classic 19th century: the curved corners of the room, the panelling and a black marble Louis XV chimney piece. This elegant upstairs living room combines traditional upholstered pieces with 1960s side chairs, a distinctly '70s shaggy rug and an arc floor light. The monochrome colour scheme adroitly unifies the disparate elements.

BARN CONVERSION

Accessed via a separate entrance, the barn, with its rustic plank-and-beam ceilings and uneven plaster walls, has an informal feel (this page). The dazzlingly bright white sitting room, overlooking the courtyard garden, is furnished for relaxation with an L-shaped arrangement of two divan/box spring beds, topped with a mass of vintage white linen cushions. Annie customized the oversized lamp shade with a coat of paint and a tassel trim.

SHADOW AND LIGHT

A textural mix of unfinished wood, chalky plaster and salvaged floorboards gives the barn landing (opposite) a raw feel that celebrates humble materials. Shapely green glass bottles on either side of the door are the only touch of colour.

Although these rooms are sparsely furnished, there are decorative touches that any amateur brocanteur would appreciate. Annie and Colin cannot resist the odd whimsical purchase from the weekly local flea market: stuffed ducks, a sculptural ceramic vessel or two, an extensive collection of cream Moustiers platters displayed on the dining-room walls and a collection of antlers add a layer of frivolity to the scheme. Despite their minimalist tendencies, the Moores are inveterate collectors who love to turn junk shopping into a game with a budget and a theme. Annie insists that they never buy anything for its provenance but will discover some pleasing object and then build a collection (until everybody else is after that particular thing and the price goes up).

The ethereally white sitting room in the barn inspired a white-themed still life that combines a Casio electronic keyboard, a white top hat, a 1950s daisy-print tea service, a white analogue telephone and a 1970s white television. Displayed in such a stylish setting, you could be persuaded that defunct electronics are the antiques of the future.

The Moores have used the barn's hallway as another opportunity for display, demonstrating that even the most humble objects can be decorative when grouped together. Walls are hung with a collection of rusted iron tools, some still in commission, others chosen for their shape or texture. Two burnished leather saddles perched on a basket of kindling help reinforce the 'country boot room' narrative.

A NEW LEAF

In the dining room, Annie used wall-to-wall pattern for the first time in her decorating career. By juxtaposing the retro leaf motif with modern shapes and materials – an oval marble-topped Saarinen table, balloon-backed chairs and a pendant shade – she has made the room look fresh and original (opposite left and above).

CREAM ON WHITE

A collection of vintage cream Moustiers platters, arranged against the leaf motif wallpaper, makes an unexpected and eye-catching display in the dining room (left).

The unlikely combination of floral-print pillows and a black-and-white cowhide ensures that the bedroom is anything but predictable. Colin made the basic wooden bed from salvaged timber, but it is rendered luxurious with a wool futon and soft linen in sophisticated shades of mauve and grey.

ALTHOUGH THESE ROOMS ARE SPARSELY
FURNISHED, THERE ARE DECORATIVE
TOUCHES THAT ANY AMATEUR BROCANTEUR
WOULD APPRECIATE.

WALLFLOWER
Annie has added a dose of retro
florals to several rooms (above).
Here, the wallpaper works as
an oversized alternative to a
headboard, framing the low bed
and bedside tables, which neatly
store a collection of paperbacks .

OUTSIDE IN
The decorative 1940s American
wrought-iron chair (right) was
made for a garden but has a found
a natural home inside the house.

ANNIE HAS DEVELOPED HER OWN STYLE OF NEATNIK COMFORT;
BEDROOMS ARE FURNISHED WITH SIMPLE WOODEN BEDS TOPPED
WITH STURDY, WOOL FUTONS.

ROOMS WITH A VIEW

A portfolio of life drawings in simple frames fills a wall of the master bedroom (above left). Colin made the four-poster bed from unfinished pine and stretched a linen canopy over the top. In the bathroom (above), a salvaged roll-top bathtub is teamed with a sleek contemporary black vanity unit fitted with a sink.

TOOLS OF THE TRADE

The entrance to the barn (overleaf, left) is decorated with a collection of vintage tools hung on the walls – beautiful as well as useful. A wire basket on castors contains kindling. Colin bought the saddle for its looks, rather than its purpose, and keeps it in the barn.

GREEN AND BLACK

Greenery of contrasting shapes fills the courtyard (previous page, right). Annie has kept to a sober colour scheme and added contemporary black garden chairs and a square black parasol. A minimalist fountain supplies the soothing background sound of trickling water.

GREEN HOUSE

An oversized hemp lampshade adds texture to the orangery (this page), where leaves trail and tumble over the chalky white walls. Stacks of terracotta pots fill the alcove.

bohemian

DEFINITION: INDIVIDUALISTS,
ICONOCLASTS, EXPLORERS,
FREE-THINKERS, ECCENTRICS.
BOHEMIANS ARE NEVER
PHASED BY LACK OF FUNDS
OR SQUARE METRES, AS THEIR
SOLUTIONS ARE ALWAYS
INVENTIVE AND ORIGINAL.

Liza
Sherman

Inventive arrangements come naturally to Liza Sherman, an original thinker whose two shops in downtown Manhattan were ahead of the curve in reinventing industrial furniture for the home. Machinist's chairs, metal shelving, ladders, photographer's lights – all find a new purpose when Liza uses them in domestic interiors, combining pieces in steel and rustic wood with ethnic textiles and collections of vintage glass and ceramics.

Liza has the retailer's approach to interior design: her stuff doesn't stay in one place for long but moves around the open-plan apartment. As the original 'canvas' wasn't working for her, she tore down five internal walls so that she could play with scale, asymmetry, colour and texture.

In the entryway, classic black-and-white tiles laid at an angle inspired Liza to set all the furniture on the bias to mimic the floor's lines and to define different areas with angled rugs. Instead of making a floor plan, she pushed the furniture around until the arrangement felt right. Trained as an artist, Liza is an iconoclast when it comes to interior design. She claims that she doesn't 'decorate' but sees objects and furniture as shapes, lines and forms that she manipulates within the space available. The 'middle layer' is Liza's name for the space between furniture and the ceiling, which she regards as another opportunity for display. Chairs hang from the office ceiling, an agricultural map of France is suspended from the ceiling in the kitchen and in the study an Anglo–Raj quilt dips below a beam.

The chartreuse-yellow bedroom is strewn with textiles collected by Liza from a variety of exotic locations. The bed, butted up against the fireplace, sports toile de Jouy cushions alongside pillows made from humble grain sacks and block-printed cotton quilts. A vintage factory shelving unit is piled with folded sarongs, saris and plaids, a cane mannequin wears a 19th-century opera coat and the coat stand is hung with an eccentric hat collection befitting a travelling theatre company.

PILE IT ON!
Neatly folded clothes are displayed on open shelves made of wire (left). Never afraid to bring different decorating genres together, Liza mixes textiles of diverse provenances on her bed (opposite): striped French grain sacks made into pillows, pastoral toile de Jouy, graphic block-printed Indian quilts and floral embroidered silks. Above the fireplace (which serves as a headboard), she has hung several antique gilded mirrors and her own portrait, employing the canny merchandiser's trick – multiples of everything.

With its yellow gloss floors, tall black window frames and primary colour palette borrowed from Dutch art movement De Stijl, Liza's home has nothing in common with the typical 'Classic 8' New York apartment that it once was. The original floor plan has been turned on its head and the space has morphed into a more appropriate artist's loft, furnished with enough textures and layers to fill a souk.

The combined living area allows Liza to parade her collections on consoles, open shelves, on top of armoires, hanging from beams, swinging from chandeliers (literally), lined up on tables, clustered on worksurfaces and piled in stacks. Surprisingly, the effect isn't as hectic as it sounds; the pop art colour combinations are diluted by plenty of black and white, the furniture arrangements are dynamic and although the space is 'open plan' the eye cannot discover everything in one glance; there are rooms within rooms here. Liza's eye is wonderfully bold and confident.

The apartment is her laboratory, a temporary landing pad for the idiosyncratic pieces that might eventually make it into her shop. Were it not for the pre-war lift/elevator, which can't accommodate anything over 2.4 metres/8 feet, the line between home and business might disappear entirely.

ON DISPLAY

The console table (above) is a vehicle for a still life of objects trawled from far-flung journeys: a silk kimono from Korea, Japanese wooden shoes, vintage palettes and a beaded headpiece from Africa.

CLUTER BUSTER

The only things that Liza likes to compartmentalize are small accessories, such as sunglasses and beads, which she loads into vintage metal trays, originally used for making sweets (opposite).

UNCOMMON ARRANGEMENTS

Liza sets up still lifes on every surface, favouring groups of large-scale, esoteric objects like the four bee skeps and the eel trap on the console table. The roughly painted walls may be white, but they are far from plain or boring. Liza keeps them interesting with a collage of oversized pieces: a framed textile alongside a scientific poster. In the corner leans a white-painted gate topped with an empty frame. The window is left bare but dressed with an African feather mandala.

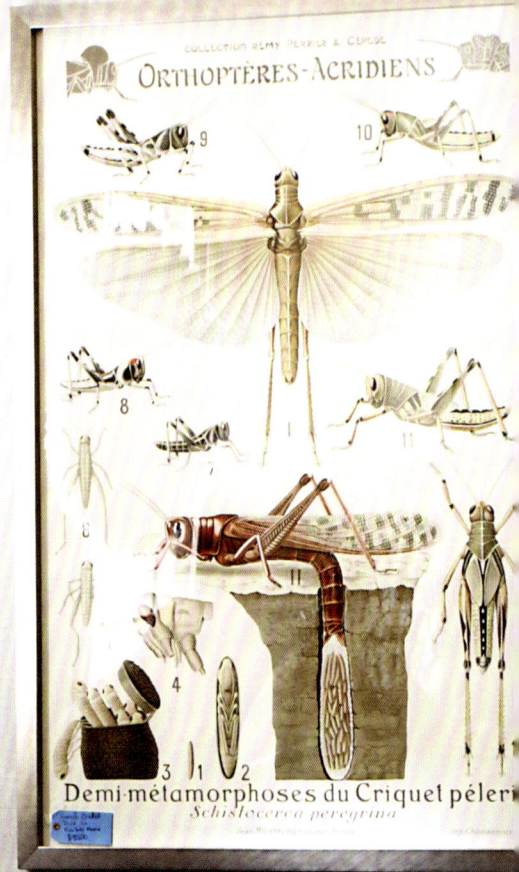

SCREENED OFF

Ethnic textiles, pharmacy bottles and glass lab ware coexist on a mismatched pair of shelf units placed at right angles to each other (left). Using these fixtures to divide the open-plan kitchen from the dining area is both practical and decorative; mixing bowls, water jugs and vases are close to hand, and the shelves work as a screen between the two zones. A tall wooden ladder offers another place to hang linens or pots and pans, which can be suspended from butcher's hooks.

IN THE MIX

Three industrial-sized electric whisks hover above the kitchen sink (opposite). In Liza's inventive world, kitchen utensils are reimagined as light fixtures, and frying pans are hung on the wall instead of art.

THIS MAGPIE COLLECTOR ALWAYS FINDS ORIGINAL WAYS TO CORRAL HER STUFF. AFTER A LIFETIME OF TRAVELLING, SHE HAS A SIGNATURE LOOK THAT FUSES ETHNIC AND INDUSTRIAL FINDS WITH ANTIQUES AND POP ART.

CAUGHT IN THE NET

Liza jazzes up her conventional white subway-tiled bathroom (opposite left) with several open-weave hessian curtains strewn with coral fronds and mother-of-pearl discs. An empty cane birdcage above the basin adds yet another note of whimsy.

HOMEWORK

In her office (above), Liza chose simple hessian panels to filter the light and soften the graphic lines of the black window frames, the vintage machinist's stool, the folding metal hospital table and the old brass desk lamp

Stephen Johnson

In certain circles, bohemianism is a lifestyle choice tied to unorthodox social and political views and living spaces that reflect a nomadic spirit. But Stephen Johnson jokes that he's merely an imposter – he's not bohemian, just cheap.

Thrift, however, isn't the reason that the photographer and art director hasn't fixed the Robert Ogden clock leaning up against the wall in his kitchen. At his house, it's always 2:32. Not because that's cocktail time, or even nap time. He's just happy to look at the numbers because he loves their shapes. Stephen is especially fond of the curves and angles of the number 2, which led him to purchase a very large painted metal version and treat it like a piece of art.

In fact, Stephen really likes round things – like the clock itself. This is a man who can find charm in a tin globe pencil sharpener picked up at a flea market. Colourful Chinese floats, a leather medicine ball, a pile of bronze coins, a big round clump of clay, dried lemons and limes – Stephen is attracted to the shape in all manner of materials. In whatever mode it comes, however, it can't be too fancy. Admittedly clumsy, he has no patience for tiptoeing around precious objects or important furnishings.

Stephen's apartment, a small, light-filled fifth-floor walk-up in Manhattan's West Village, is filled with humble collections treated with great aplomb. Along with wonderful orbs arranged on tables, corralled in boxes and displayed on shelves, he manages to turn a collection of chipped and rusting metal boxes into a painterly assemblage. The nautical wall – there's a chart of knots glued to an ocean-blue piece of cardboard, a hand-drawn nautilus shell, framed blowfish illustrations torn from a book, a foreboding oil of a tumultuous midnight sea and a pair of ocean-blue tiles – suggests that Stephen will eventually cover it entirely. And then there's 'moonman', Stephen's beloved talisman (and Instagram handle), standing guard on a shelf stacked with 1970s milk-glass yogurt containers and reproduced in an outsized half-tone print hung over his bed.

A KIND OF BLUE

In Stephen's tiny apartment it made sense to restrict the colour palette to his favourite shades of blue, together with a few moody greys. The longest wall in the living room (above) is hung with a mix of artworks that share the palette and the themes that Stephen returns to time after time – nautical knots, a seascape, Planet Earth, a black-and-white print of blowfish, a tin globe, a number 2 – assembled in a layered montage.

THIS IS A MAN WHO CAN FIND CHARM IN A TIN GLOBE
PENCIL SHARPENER PICKED UP AT A FLEA MARKET.

The astronaut's stance in the grainy photo strikes Stephen as shy yet curious, not unlike his partner John Derian, the artist and owner of two eponymous Manhattan shops, whose fingerprints can be subtly detected in each and every room. The pair share a love for the tatty and the tumbledown, but Stephen, who describes himself as the most feminine man on the planet, just happens to love masculine objects and palettes. He tidily sums up where their aesthetic diverges with a single example: Derian loves neutrals and chintz, Stephen does not. Awash in moody blue tones, each of Stephen's rooms features a dominant colour that's reminiscent of the sea and sky. And, as if to impose perfect angles that are missing from the rooms themselves, Stephen spent a full weekend stencilling a graphic, tessellated Escheresque pattern in his favourite palette on the apartment's floor.

Such a rigorous floor design might suggest that Stephen holds on a bit too tight. But his sense of humour is also on full display, not least in the form of poultry. Lauren Bacock, the stuffed chicken he rescued from the Chelsea flea market and promptly took to chic bistro Balthazar for lunch, stands watch over his collections in the living room, while an almost life-size ceramic plucked chicken by Astier de Villatte, a gift from John, permanently and patiently awaits its fate on a platter on the kitchen counter.

ROUND AND AROUND
Vignettes on every surface in Stephen's apartment involve orbs of some kind. Framed illustrations of blowfish are propped up on the radiator (above left), while an alcove, stacked with metal boxes for storage and magazines, features a découpage eye plate by John Derian (above right). Lauren Bacock, the stuffed chicken, perches here too. As a contrast to the black and blue, Stephen has chosen a jolt of scarlet in a simple painted desk chair and a tiny elephant figure (opposite).

WORLD EXPLORER

A glass box (this page) contains favourite totems: spheres, a paper heart, a tiny hammer from an action figure and a lump of fool's gold, assembled on a ceramic tile. Stephen translated the tile's Escheresque pattern meticulously onto the floor.

OUTER SPACE

Above his bed, Stephen has hung a large digital print of 'moonman', a character to whom he is obsessively drawn for his optimism and curiosity. A collection of spherical objects, including a leather medicine ball, a tin globe and a metallic spotlight, crowds the plinth used as a bedside table (opposite). Hanging low above it is a utilitarian white metal shade.

Alina
Preciado

Alina Preciado, a professional bohemian and
traveller (albeit one with neatnik tendencies),
lives in an edgy up-and-coming neighbourhood
in Brooklyn, as any self-respecting NY bohemian
should. Her apartment has all the features of a
classic loft: concrete floors, scarred and burnished
by years of use, and metal-framed factory windows
with the original industrial grime still intact.
All manner of pipes and ducts snake around the
ceiling; there's a big concrete column holding
the ceiling up and a huge, clunky metal door.

When Alina first moved into the space, previously a carpenter's
workshop, some 11 years ago, it was full of wood and tools.
She salvaged some of the wood, scraped multiple layers of
gunk off the floor and then sat back and thought about how
she wanted to live here.

When she had worked out exactly how the light shifted
from morning to night, she built herself a sort of open box
to sleep in. Tucked to one side of the space, it has curtains
that can be pulled for privacy or whenever she doesn't want
to watch the dramatic shaft of light travel across the room.

Other than a bathroom bisecting one end of the loft, a
storage room and a walk-in wardrobe, the layout is entirely
open plan. Alina has devised zones for different activities: the
living area stationed next to the longest stretch of windows
on the south side is defined by a symmetrical arrangement of
two dove-grey armchairs opposite a sofa, three low Moroccan
silver metal-clad tea tables and a couple of ottomans sitting
on top of layered cowhides. A combination of sunlight and
a wood-burning stove warms this living room within a room.
There's an East-meets-West mix of things in sophisticated
neutrals that characterizes Alina's style – 'contemporary
urban gypsy' seems to sum it up.

LOFTY IDEAS

Alina has divided her classic New York loft into different zones. The living area is defined by a symmetrical arrangement of two armchairs, a contemporary black leather sofa and two layered cowhides in white and speckled grey. A group of three low, engraved metal Moroccan tea tables brings an exotic edge to the scene. Embroidered leather poufs provide extra seating and amp up the sophisticated souk vibe.

SORTED

Alina has many systems
for keeping her possessions
organized. She has an
assortment of baskets by the
front door (this page), each
containing something that she
needs to take out with her:
dry cleaning, for example, or
library books, hats and gloves.
Over time, she has gathered a
mismatched selection of hooks,
which are fixed to the wall. The
vintage index-card cabinet next
to the window (opposite) holds
office sundries.

The functional, unfitted kitchen, positioned next to another stretch of windows, consists of open stainless-steel shelves, sourced from an industrial kitchen specialist, a black stove and a salvaged enamel sink and double drainer, opposite a vintage carpenter's bench. Serving as both worksurface and island, this divides the kitchen from the dining area. Alina keeps plates, glasses and pots all to hand, either on the shelves or hanging from butcher's hooks on a rail. More or less everything coordinates in this haven of monochrome (even her two cats are striped in shades of grey, black and taupe), but hints of silver, copper, bronze and gold introduce a dose of femininity and exoticism, tempering the hard edges of the building's industrial rawness.

Much of the tableware assembled in neat rows along the shelves – tactile Colombian ceramics, Moroccan glasses and chopping boards – has been sourced by Alina for her own online store, aptly named *Dar Gitane* (Gypsy Home). Next to the stove, there's a stoneware pot bursting with a comprehensive collection of seasoned wooden utensils gathered from buying trips and local flea markets.

Further investigation reveals that exotic travel is the preoccupation that connects everything here. Alina has turned one wall into a huge 3-D mood board hung with everything from pieces of feather trim to antique textiles, such as a 1930s French brassiere and a Berber face mask.

White-painted frames without their glass hold clusters of miniature objects that can't be hung with drawing pins; a clutch of vintage purses is housed in one of these frames. As she likes to use these accessories, Alina keeps them on display by her desk rather than hidden in a drawer. Similarly, by the front door she has gathered together a collection of market baskets suspended from metal hooks. Each basket has a purpose: clothes for the dry cleaner in one, books to return to the library in another, gloves and scarves ready to grab on sorties into the outside world folded into a further one.

Opposite her desk, Alina has arranged a tableau of precious pieces beneath glass cloches: a silk Mongolian child's boot, an incense holder and brass vials of kohl eyeliner from India are each singled out as objects to appreciate, conjuring memories of past journeys or suggesting ideas for future ones.

SPICE ROUTE

Alina divided the kitchen from
the dining area with a vintage
carpenter's workbench, which
is in keeping with the loft's past
as a workshop (opposite right).
When she's at home, she likes to
cook using spices (opposite left),
discovered on buying trips for her
online shop, *Dar Gitane*.

TO DINE FOR

On the other side of the counter,
a long dining table seating eight
(this page) is near enough for
Alina to hang out with guests and
chat while she cooks. The abstract
painting is by Joseph Maruska and
the tubular aluminium wall lights
were found at a local flea market.

The hyper-organized kitchen was put together with a few simple, unfitted elements that work stylishly together. Alina found the robust stainless-steel shelves at a catering supply shop on the Bowery, New York. Glasses, tea canisters, pots, casseroles and dishes are all kept close to hand, displayed in rows along the shelves.

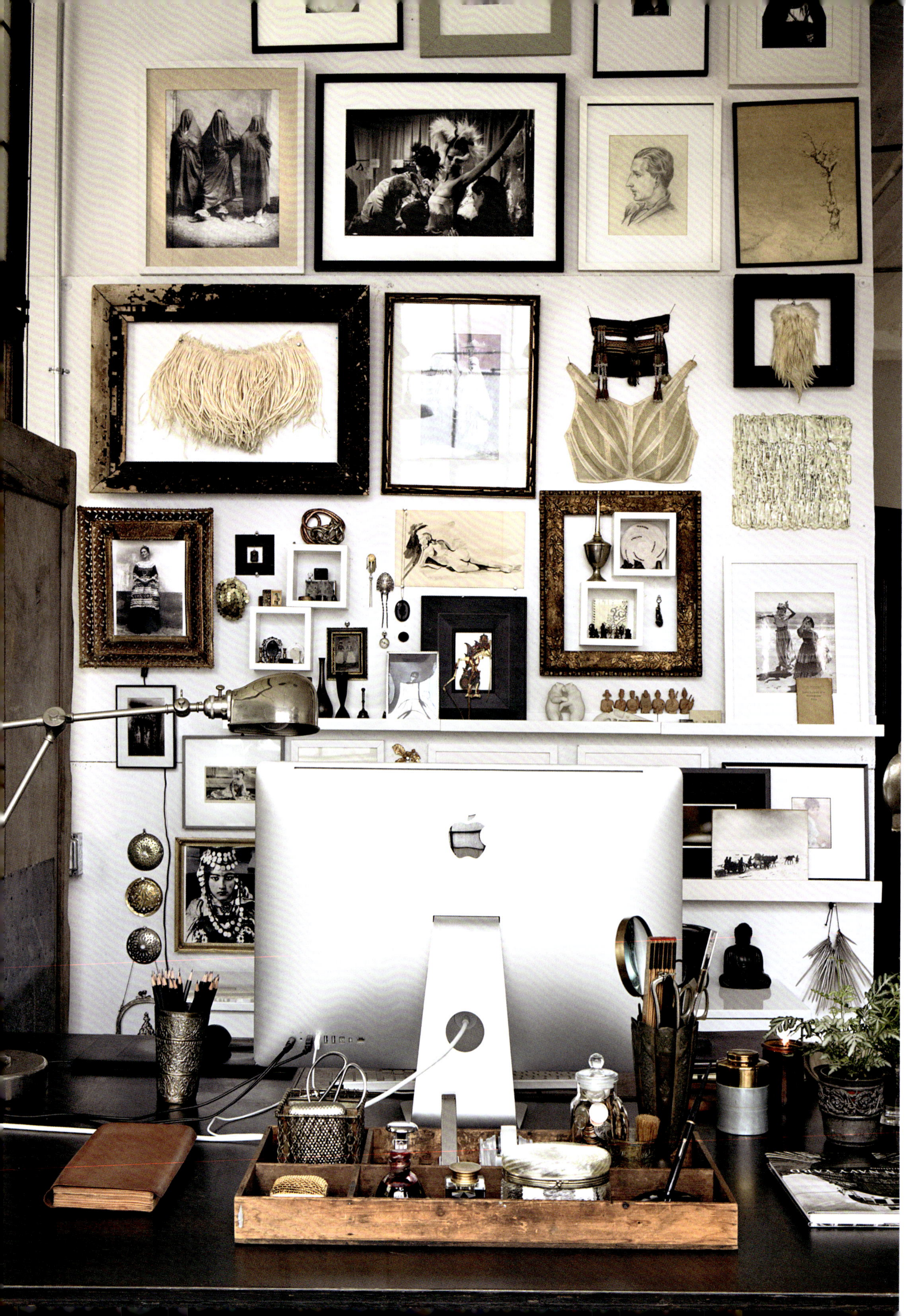

MOOD BOARD

Alina uses the wall behind her desk (opposite) as a 3-D mood board with product-development ideas for her business. Samples, pages from magazines, *objets trouvés*, framed photographs, antique textiles and interesting hardware are all corralled onto one surface with drawing pins or propped up on shallow white shelves. Many of the black-and-white photos are from a project on veils that Alina put together for her masters degree.

TRAY CHIC

A wooden tray divided into sections holds desk accessories that are used everyday (above). Instead of tucking them into a drawer, Alina keeps her collection of vintage clutch bags and purses, from the 1920s, '30s and '40s, next to her desk so that she doesn't forget to use them (right).

THERE'S AN EAST-MEETS-WEST MIX OF THINGS IN SOPHISTICATED NEUTRALS THAT CHARACTERIZES ALINA'S STYLE – 'CONTEMPORARY URBAN GYPSY' SEEMS TO SUM IT UP.

BOXED IN

Rather than building full-height dividing walls, Alina had the idea of designing an open box to use as her bedroom (above). Whenever she wants privacy, she can pull across the curtains that close off two aspects of the structure.

BATHING BEAUTY

Although most of the loft is open plan, Alina divided the office area from the kitchen with a small enclosed room that's her bathroom. The salvaged roll-top bathtub is where Alina can relax and sample the scented oils, candles and incense that she sources from all over the world (opposite). Ferns and other plants thrive in the steamy atmosphere, and there is a tiny sink in the utility area of the loft that's devoted to watering potted herbs (right).

naturalist

DEFINITION: BEACHCOMBERS,
FORAGERS, FLOWER PEOPLE,
DISCIPLES OF THOREAU. LOVERS
OF NATURE WHO WANT TO
BRING THE OUTSIDE IN.

Charlotte Vadum

Danish designer Charlotte Vadum likes to mix rough with smooth in her collections. Her flair for giving luxe fabrics a rock-and-roll edge has become a hallmark of her brand, in which the clothing is cut in clean shapes from strong graphic prints influenced by modern art, music and street life. Rich silks and cashmere are mixed with washed-out cottons and leather, unexpected combinations that she likes to think bring her collections alive. The women who wear her clothes love them because they're, well, cool.

It's not surprising, then, that her 'summer house' – the country retreat that Charlotte shares with her husband Jens and daughters Carla and Viola – exudes a similar vibe, a yin and yang that's so perfectly calibrated that the richness never outshines the roughness, the new is stealthily combined with the second-hand, and a modern sensibility doesn't upstage an appreciation of vintage pieces. The bijou L-shaped getaway, a mere 75 square metres/800 square feet in size, is just a swift 45-minute drive from central Copenhagen and the fourth-floor apartment where the family permanently resides.

THE L-SHAPED HOME

Charlotte's coastal escape is an L-shaped, one-storey home built in the 1960s. The interior walls and the floorboards have all been painted white, making the space into a bright, light backdrop for Charlotte to decorate with her mid-century furniture and textiles (this page and opposite), as well as accessories, in her favourite monochrome palette.

GALLERY STYLE

Charlotte says that she prefers to see colour in nature rather than interiors, and feels her monochrome decor allows the colours of the natural world outside to take centre stage. She sticks to black-and-white art too, and collects Danish artist Sikker Hansen's work from the 1930s and '40s. The longest wall in the house is hung 'salon' style with paintings that Charlotte has found at flea markets.

Set in an acre of land just minutes from the seashore, the single-storey clapboard cottage is a world away from busy city life. Every single weekend from April to November (and occasionally in the winter months, when there's enough snow to ski on the nearby hills), Charlotte and her family are lured away from their metropolitan lives to a more primitive place, as Charlotte likes to describe it.

The design of the flat-roofed 1960s building is simplicity itself, but in Charlotte's hands it has ended up looking rather sophisticated. Painted black on the outside, it merges discreetly with the surrounding pine woods, while inside Charlotte has bathed almost every single surface – walls, ceilings and floors – in crisp white. To give the place texture,

she has filled it with lots of wood, ceramics and treasures picked up at the beach and on country walks. A fan of 1960s and '70s design, Charlotte spends most weekends at the local flea market, where she hunts for 'typical' pottery from the period that looks anything but when arranged against a slick white background. Walls are adorned with a collection of black-and-white art, hung 'salon' style, and instead of a sofa there are daybeds strewn with fleeces and textural blankets. A clutch of carved wooden stars strung together on twine looks like sculpture floating against a lonely white wall, and Charlotte manages to make even the most clichéd elements of coastal living – starfish, shells, rocks – look interesting again, by mixing them with decidedly modern elements.

Nature provides a lush contrast to the monochrome scheme; oversized windows flood the rooms with light and enough shades of green to tame the bold colour contrasts inside. In the warmer months, four huge doors, leading onto a decked terrace and a low-maintenance potted garden, stand open for most of the time. Guests stay in a self-contained bedroom in a black-painted wooden hut in the garden.

Charlotte admits that she never tires of the monochrome scheme, a sentiment her daughters do not share. They love spinning the colour wheel, a fact Charlotte manages to embrace by remembering her devotion to contradiction. She sees their bedroom – with its floral wallpaper and patchwork quilt – as giving the interior a good dose of humour. The coverlet squares, knitted from leftover yarns collected from traditional knitters all over Denmark, is particularly pleasing to Charlotte, not only for its humble source but also its soul.

OPEN PLAN

A 1960s vintage sideboard provides useful storage and somewhere to display vintage ceramics. The colour of the oak leaves echoes the greeny black glaze on the squat, cylindrical pot, and the round tray is printed with a tree pattern.

DAYDREAMING

Instead of a sofa, Charlotte has placed two daybeds at right angles to each other and added texture in the form of sheepskins, throws and cushions. Favourite objects are grouped along the window ledge, and on the side table is a cluster of vessels with interesting textures and shapes.

HERE, THE NEW IS STEALTHILY COMBINED WITH THE SECOND-HAND, AND A MODERN SENSIBILITY DOESN'T UPSTAGE AN APPRECIATION OF VINTAGE PIECES.

GALLEY KITCHEN

The house has four points of entry, and one door opens into the kitchen, with its simple white walls and matt black units (above right). Charlotte has accessorized the space with tableware from the 1950s and '60s, much of it bought from local flea markets (above left). Carved wooden stars strung together on a length of twine make a decorative sculpture (left).

SPACE SAVING

A space-saving storage bench running down one side of the dining table is teamed with a stool and two functional plywood and tubular steel chairs (opposite). Despite her strict adherence to a monochrome scheme, Charlotte could not resist a splash of acid yellow in the shape of an enamel jug and a glass pitcher.

BLACK LOOKS

While the interior of the house is white, the exterior is painted black, which works wonderfully with the surrounding foliage. As she uses the house mostly at weekends, Charlotte has planted a low-maintenance garden with pots of grasses, herbs, coppery heuchera and chocolate cosmos (this page). There is enough privacy at the front of the house for a black table and chairs (opposite), which are almost camouflaged by the weatherboard walls.

Lindsey Taylor

Garden designer Lindsey Taylor has something that seasoned New Yorkers covet: a penthouse with a rooftop terrace that also comes with a key to the lush gardens in Gramercy Park, Manhattan's only remaining private patch of green. Eleven floors up, her 46-square-metre/ 500-square-foot studio room with a view may be diminutive, but it opens onto a plant-filled wraparound garden. Bent on extending her oasis, Lindsey has managed to blur the boundary between exterior and interior by introducing all manner of natural stuff inside as well as out.

Thriving, dying, dead, bronzed, painted, woven, thrown, sculpted, fossilized – Lindsey's passion for nature and the organic shapes that it inspires shows up in every way and on every surface, in arrangements that are as spontaneous as Mother Nature herself. A handsome black cabinet provides the ground for a classic Taylor tableau: willowy branches of foliage make an arrangement in themselves, while a vintage flower frog acts as armature for an installation of black pussy willow stems, dried David Austin roses and a Polaroid of the buds at a more vibrant stage. What isn't tucked into vases and vessels is framed – a piece of Maine seaweed, a favourite painting of a bird, painted stems and a perfect little landscape preside over it all. Along the narrow fireplace mantel, Lindsey has thoughtfully strewn treasured beach finds and sentimental reminders of a lifetime of travel.

No surface is spared Lindsey's pottery obsession, a passion that has grown over the two decades since she began acquiring pieces with the same instinctive spirit that is evident throughout the space. Ask her about the many early Atwater pieces she gave away to friends before they became coveted by collectors, and her response is tinged with wistful regret. Frances Palmer, Joan Platt, Eva Zeisel, Paula Greif, Whiteforth, Jars, Kara Hamilton, Nancy Bosch – Lindsey is as conversant in potters and ceramicists of both indie and international renown as she is in plant species.

Limiting the palette to neutrals, black and white allows Lindsey to play with shapes and glazes; an exuberant, glossy Eva Zeisel teapot plays up the earthy beauty of the pieces surrounding it. A bronze sycamore pod on the mantel gets all the attention at first glance, but the sea branches tucked into

SHOEHORNED

Entering Lindsey Taylor's penthouse apartment is a novel experience, as the front door swings open into a tiny kitchen squeezed into the vestibule. Nearly black paint (Railings by Farrow & Ball) is a smart backdrop for a diverse array of kitchenalia. Every nook and cranny is put to good use: knives line up along a magnetic strip on the wall, the windowsill is crammed with vessels containing spoons and spatulas and narrow shelves in a shallow alcove are stacked with cups and glasses (opposite and above left).

the raku mugs behind it are what keep you there. Indeed, Lindsey is more interested in shape, form, texture and colour than in provenance, which is why she's just as enamoured of the dainty pinch pot made by her husband, furniture designer Joseph Fratesi of Atlas Industries, as she is of her 18th-century French ceramic teacups.

Despite the density of the collections, the space has a quiet, minimal vibe thanks to a wall of practical floor-to-ceiling cabinets hiding Lindsey's more mundane possessions. The tiny black-painted kitchen, shoehorned into the entrance, may be tightly packed with kitchenalia, but it makes a graphic counterpoint to the light-filled room beyond.

ONLY NATURAL

Lindsey has strewn one end of her mantelpiece (opposite left) with a collection of flora and fauna gathered on beach and forest walks. At the other end, she switches to a wildlife theme, with a band of animal figures (just seen above).

TABLESCAPE

On the dining table, instead of the conventional vase of flowers, Lindsey has opted for a broad Scandinavian art glass bowl by Orrefors filled to the brim with plump pink radishes (above). Her sleek, emerald-green, marble-topped table is the one streak of colour in the neutral setting, teamed with versatile glossy black bentwood chairs.

THE NEW BASICS COOKBOOK
COOKIES
Birds
500
SIBLEY GUIDE
Ireland
CROW LAKE
BAKING HANDBOOK
MARTHA STEWART'S COOKING SCHOOL
TAMASIN'S KITCHEN BIBLE
Tender
grasses
David Hockney Portraits
Calder Jewelry
Francis Bacon
VELAZQUEZ
Vincent van Gogh
MANET
GEORGES SEURAT THE DRAWINGS
THE PRADO
Painting People
MORANDI
Lucian Freud
SELTZER

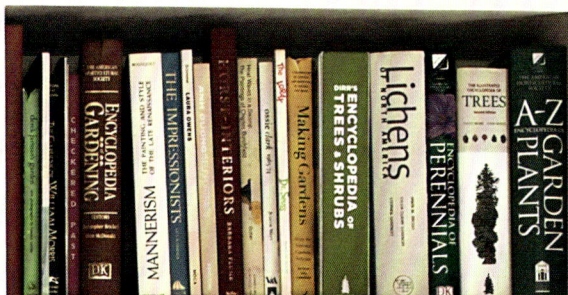

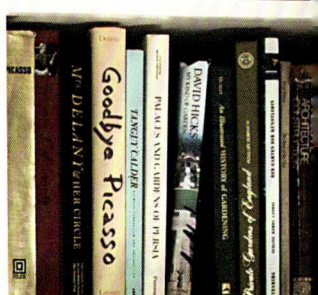

CONCEAL AND REVEAL

Devoting a whole wall to built-in storage makes it possible to live in a tiny apartment without sacrificing a sense of style. Open shelves reaching up to the ceiling contain books, while the lower spaces are the perfect spot to display Lindsey's collection of ceramics by US potters, including Frances Palmer, Paula Greif, Atwater and Joan Platt. Her office hardware and her sound system are also slotted in here.

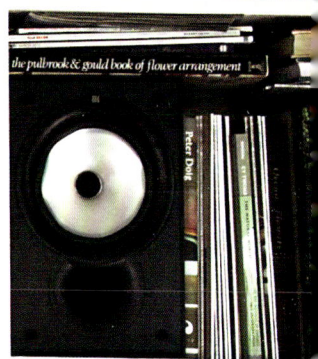

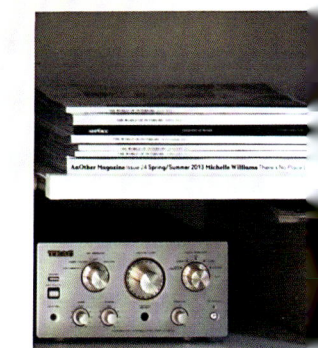

THRIVING, DYING, DEAD, BRONZED, PAINTED, WOVEN, THROWN, SCULPTED, FOSSILIZED – LINDSEY'S PASSION FOR NATURE AND THE ORGANIC SHAPES THAT IT INSPIRES IS EVIDENT THROUGHOUT HER APARTMENT.

STILL LIFE FROM NATURE

Lindsey is drawn to the subtle colours and textures found in nature and holds onto dried branches, rose petals and leaves, incorporating them into still lifes (above). Working on flower arrangements for photo shoots means that she visits New York's garden district (a short stroll from her home) several times a week.

INDIVIDUAL

Handmade, organic-shaped bowls and cups are something that Lindsey finds difficult to resist – she prefers to eat and drink from hand-crafted pieces. Her grandmother's weathered pewter platter is used as a tray for green tea served in a pinched-pottery cup (opposite).

sculpture vulture

DEFINITION: ART LOVERS WITH A LOVE FOR SCULPTURAL OBJECTS PLACED JUST SO, SCULPTURE VULTURES HAVE A CONNOISSEUR'S EYE AND ARE MIX-MASTERS FOR WHOM PROPORTION IS EVERYTHING.

Charles van Mitty

When Charles van Mitty was working on his series of *Sharp and Dangerous Objects*, among his installations was a series of axes dangling from the ceiling. He had been making hanging art for decades, noting that most of the people he knew had no wall space left. The pointy, threatening period, however, happened to coincide with his children's toddlerhood. When one of the hatchets broke free and embedded itself in the floor, his wife Alexandra wisely suggested he dismantle the piece and focus on his other passion, painting.

That was almost two decades ago, and while Charles still makes paintings at the family's home in Manhattan, where the world of finance commands his days, he never gave up on his passion for wire, wood, metal, stone and scavenged objects. Instead, he took it upstate to New York's Schoharie County, where, in one of the barns behind the Federal Colonial home that he shares with his wife and now-grown son and daughter, hundreds of curiously beautiful objects, both spiky and otherwise, are assembled, reassembled or simply artfully arranged on the long tables and wooden shelves that line its walls and two floors.

Built in 1840 to house one of the area's first and largest herds of sheep, the archetypical red farm building now serves as Charles van Mitty's Barn of Unfinished Projects, where the vast space is his to put 'everything that fits'. This includes 34-kg/75-pound rocks shipped from the beaches of his wife's native Normandy, as well as metal machinery and tools hauled east from old mining sites in the Rockies.

For the born and bred New Yorker, living a dual life comes naturally. Born into an extended family of artists and collectors – his father, a film-maker and painter, was a CBS executive – Charles had the benefit of witnessing what he calls the 'dangers' of solely pursuing a single occupation. So he split the difference, and has long been content to make

BARN AGAIN

This archetypal red barn is Charles van Mitty's Barn of Unfinished Projects – 550 square metres/6000 square feet of space to put 'everything that fits' (left). Less typical of the local vernacular are the huge, multicoloured painted sliding doors – evidence of Charles's obsession with artist Paul Klee.

SCENESTER

In the upper gallery of the barn, an unfinished chess game sits atop a giant wooden spool and sets a scene that's worthy of a Tim Burton movie (opposite).

art for his own pleasure. He has mounted shows, the most memorable in which he gave each guest two of his pieces on the condition that they must be displayed in their homes and not relegated to the attic or basement. Should this become their fate, the pieces were to be returned.

If Charles was born with a gene for making art, living in lower Manhattan in the 1970s brought it to life. He lived in Tribeca in an era when the streets were ripe for scavenging and spacious lofts were easy to come by. While his crowd – artists who worked in advertising – gradually blurred the line between the two, Charles was busy finding the potential in kerbside cast-offs, ever interested in how objects interrelate.

Tattered cigar boxes, twig chairs, vintage postal scales, cable spools, a soaring eagle that once sat atop a weathervane, a model metal staircase, a selection of smooth stones and huge stones, a porcelain egg, old shoemaker's tools – Charles's only criteria for adding to his collection are shapes and forms that please his eye. Consider the living installation that curently occupies the 2-metre/7-foot science lab table in the living room. The composition, created from an Indian grinding tool, a hornets' nest, a set of antique keys, a tin-lined gourd, a tortoise shell and the old shoe that Charles found buried in the wall of the main house – a gesture by the original builders to bring good luck to the house and its inhabitants – is the poetic work of a hunter-gatherer.

For Charles van Mitty, the pleasure is in the process; he just can't stop piling it on. His paintings, inspired by Paul Klee's 'magic squares', involve more than 20 layers, each one sanded and scratched before the next is added. They line the walls in both city and country, as well as the sliding door on the barn. He can't leave well enough alone either. Only an artist uninterested in finishing would reassemble a linear stone wall into a serpentine shape. Instead of cutting a few dead trees down to the roots, Charles left 45 cm/ 18 inches of each trunk standing, then painstakingly sculpted them with a chainsaw in the spirit of sculptor Constantin Brancusi's Endless Column. But perhaps the most alluring installation is tucked away in an entirely different outbuilding on the property. Inside, the complete contents of a dismantled barn are stacked to the rafters.

CURIOUSER AND CURIOUSER

All manner of things appeal to Charles's scavenging instincts.
In the barn, a workbench is alive with a random installation of
curious objects. Some are reassembled or combined, others just
'found' and displayed as they are (opposite).

BALANCING ACT

Charles van Mitty's repeated experiments with Klee's 'magic square'
paintings line up along the wall of the barn, creating the feel
of a studio (above). The surfaces of these works are sanded and
scratched over and over again to achieve complex patches of colour.
Sections of columns and wooden shapes are balanced one on top of
the other to make totem poles reminiscent of Brancusi's work, and
a rocking metal garden bench has been commandeered as a sofa.

SLIDE SHOW

A collection of botanical slides hung on the living room wall (right)
has a graphic quality and colour palette shared with Charles's
'square' paintings.

RAW MATERIALS

Nothing escapes Charles, who voraciously hunts and gathers discarded objects everywhere from upstate flea markets to Manhattan kerbsides. A leaning collage of slabs of wood in differing shapes and sizes becomes something appealing in itself (left).

HUNG UP

Apart from the assemblages filling the shelves, there are hanging arrangements of hooks and wires, bedsprings and pulley wheels that become impromptu mobiles in Charles's hands (below). On the top shelf (opposite), miniature versions of Brancusi's Endless Column jostle with a host of other pieces waiting for transformation.

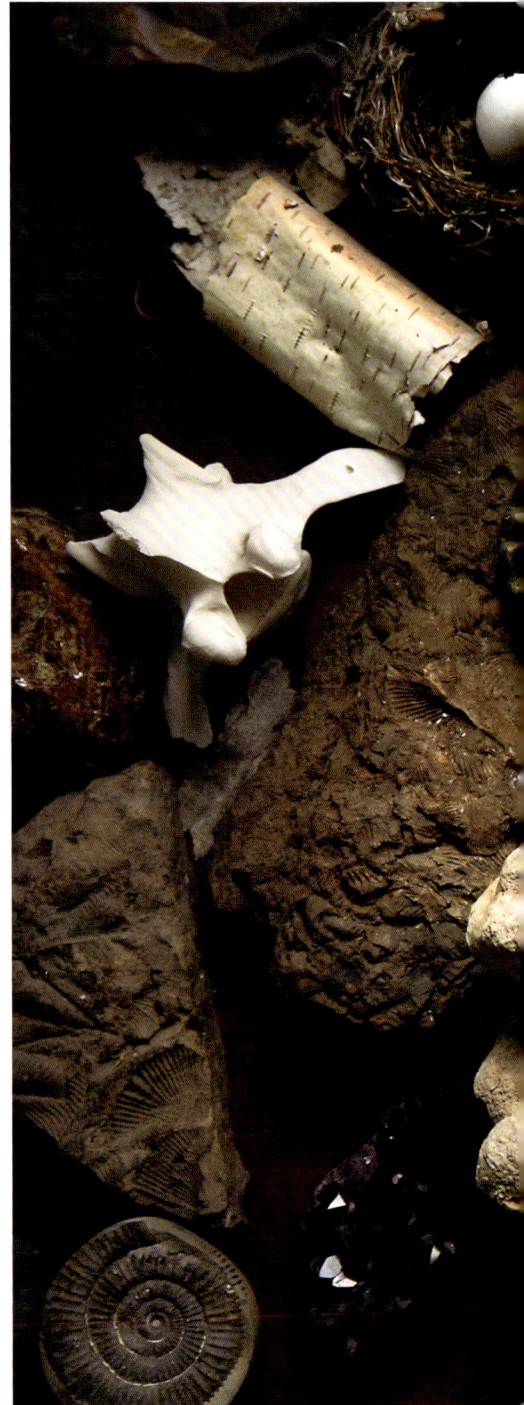

TATTERED CIGAR BOXES, TWIG CHAIRS, VINTAGE POSTAL SCALES, CABLE SPOOLS, AN EAGLE THAT ONCE SAT ATOP A WEATHERVANE, A MODEL STAIRCASE, A PORCELAIN EGG, OLD SHOEMAKER'S TOOLS – CHARLES'S ONLY CRITERIA FOR ADDING TO HIS COLLECTION ARE SHAPES AND FORMS THAT PLEASE HIS EYE.

KITCHEN EXHIBITS

In the living room of the house, on a 2-metre/7-foot-long science lab table (above), Charles has composed an installation involving items that might be described as being in a state of disintegration, as if recently excavated from the ground: an Indian grinding tool, a hornets' nest, a set of antique keys, a tin-lined gourd, a tortoise shell and an old shoe he found buried deep in the wall of the main house.

NOTED

These neatly bundled notebooks are another example of once-useful objects that have been transformed by time into something appreciated for their tactile form rather than their content (opposite left).

CHARLES'S PAINTINGS INVOLVE MORE THAN 20 LAYERS, EACH ONE SANDED AND SCRATCHED BEFORE THE NEXT IS ADDED. THEY LINE THE WALLS IN BOTH CITY AND COUNTRY, AS WELL AS THE SOARING SLIDING DOOR ON THE BARN.

COLLECTOR'S WORKS

White walls, painted white beams and a glossy white floor are the unusual context for Early American Rustic style, with an old meat safe, spindle-back Windsor chairs, collections of early wooden bowls and kitchen tools and an array of glass pitchers of every shape and size; plain, etched and pressed (opposite and left).

QUIET SUBVERSION

While the dining room, with its pewter candlesticks and glass decanters, seems to be the epitome of quiet American Federal style, some characteristic touches of whimsy have crept in: a water pitcher is full of multicoloured rubber balls and a découpage eye on a postcard from John Derian keeps watch over the table (above). On the wall, Paul Mutimear's photographs seem abstract but in fact document the movements of moths in darkness.

Bea Mombaers

There are a lot of Belgian jokes. There's also Tintin, *frites* with mayonnaise, the Antwerp Six and exemplary Art Nouveau, but even so Belgium isn't the first place that design aficionados would consider visiting for a life-enhancing dose of Chic. But, mark my words, Belgium is the new Scandinavia. There are, of course, lots of very chic Belgians who already know this and hardly need my validation, as they are too busy wearing deconstructed sweaters and Martin Margiela for Converse sneakers, and thriving stylishly at the epicentre of Northern European postmodern Chic.

When you have had too much French whimsy, Scandinavian pragmatism or Italian elaboration, head to Knokke-le-Zoute on the coast for a tonic. Apparently it's the Hamptons of Northern Europe. Interior designer, store owner and weathervane for all things stylish, Bea Mombaers always installs herself here for the summer season, when fashion and design folk flock to the resort to kick back in the Butterfly and Verner Panton chairs scattered around her garden, to sip rosé at the elongated outdoor picnic table or to potter around town on the pillar box-red bicycles that happen to be on hand for guests. Bea runs her sprawling matt black house as a B&B (albeit one that feels like a house party), but also as a showroom for the sculptural objects, rugs, lighting and furniture that she sells at a her nearby shop as well as her other store in Brussels. It's a convenient and pleasurable way for the captive design plutocrats to do their interiors shopping, and gives Bea the opportunity to show her exquisite wares working their magic in a capacious architect-designed space.

The colours of Bea's home are as sober as a nun's habit: after the forbidding black exterior, with its gabled and thatched roof (on first appearance, surely home to a modern-day fairytale witch?), there's the gritty concrete shell of an interior. The walls may be as uniformly leaden as the winter sky over the Flanders fields and the windows severe black metal grids, but the Brutalist bunker look is softened by layers of expensively sculpted sheepskin rugs, low-slung buttery leather sofas and rough linens that started life as 19th-century grain sacks and which have been reinvented as giant floor cushions. The eye is constantly working to take

SHELL LIFE

Bea Mombaers' seaside home is not only a stylish guesthouse, it is also a showcase for her skilful eye. Thick walnut shelves in the living room display objects selected to work with the monochrome colour scheme (opposite). At the end of the summer, Bea restyles the rooms with a cache of new vases, framed photographs, candlesticks, bowls and books. She is drawn to iconic pieces of furniture like the white 4801 chair by Joe Colombo for Kartell. The whole interior has grey concrete walls (above left) finished with a painted white stripe instead of skirting/baseboards, and black-framed factory-style windows with deep metal sills.

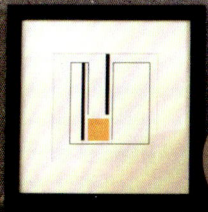

in every voluptuous curve of a ceramic vessel, classic Hans
Wegner chair, state-of-the-art lighting fixture, cast organic
form and geometric wire *objet* arranged along several chunky
walnut shelves. It's all very seductive, that blend of rough
and smooth, dark and light.

The voluminous living room is open plan, divided
from the kitchen by an island around which there is much
late-night discussion of Nightshop, the latest art opening
downtown, as the patrons perch on Charlotte Perriand bar
stools or slide around the time-worn chestnut leather of
the sturdy vintage gymnasium horse. Naturally, the kitchen
shelves are loaded with an eclectic line-up of tableware:
oversized free-form olive wood salad bowls, handmade
ceramic plates in every shade of neutral, horn ladles,
bamboo-handled cutlery, fistfuls of carved bone and wooden
spoons jutting out of terracotta jugs like primitive bunches
of flowers. Such rigorously sourced things are much too
attractive to put away in a cupboard. Bea and her sister
make stylish entertaining look effortless and casual with
this Flintstone-inflected library of props.

As you would expect, bedrooms here are indulgent and
luxurious, cave-like in their crepuscular gloom. Bea has
warmed them up with collections of richly coloured Suzani
cushions and Indian patterned quilts hung as curtains on thin
iron poles at the windows. There are clusters of shapely clay
vases gathered on mid-century sideboards and chests, and
deep windowsills piled high with books about travel, art
and interiors. Bathrooms are not separate but seamlessly
integrated with the bedrooms, equipped with cast terrazzo
bathtubs and walk-in showers. Accessories are kept on display
rather than hidden; handwoven Turkish towels hang from
leaning ladders and soaps are piled into rough cork bowls.

Every wide corridor, windowsill and light-flooded corner
provides an opportunity for Bea to exhibit to best advantage
some intriguing object or sculpture, or to lean a framed
photograph or two nonchalantly against a wall. Visitors
passing through must tussle with the constant temptation to
scoop things up and take them home. Because they can. By
next season the stage set will remain the same but the props
will have changed. Belgian style is a serious business after all.

LOW SLUNG

The view of lush green bamboo from the living room windows is like a vast abstract painting in a space where objects take precedence over pictures (left). All the furniture in the living area is low and close to the floor, so the eye has an uninterrupted view of objects and architecture. Metal, rope and leather are combined in the iconic Flag Halyard chair by Hans Wegner. A round, solid wood coffee table is stacked with interiors magazines, books and a group of free-form copper bowls (above). The club chair stationed next to it is dressed up with a black-and-white long-haired sheepskin sourced from a local herd.

CORNERED

Bea's long open-plan kitchen is where guests congregate for buffet breakfasts and coffees throughout the day. Shelves are stacked with tactile ceramics in every shade of neutral, while cutlery/flatware is stored in jars and cups (above left and opposite below).

A LONG STORY

The breakfast bar separates the living room from the kitchen, defining the zone behind it as the work space (above right). Charlotte Perriand leather bar stools and a vintage gymnasium horse line up alongside it so that guests can perch here and socialize while Bea and her sister prepare food and drinks.

BEA RUNS HER SPRAWLING MATT BLACK HOUSE AS A B&B (ALBEIT ONE THAT FEELS LIKE A HOUSE PARTY), BUT ALSO AS A SHOWROOM FOR THE SCULPTURAL OBJECTS, RUGS, LIGHTING AND FURNITURE THAT SHE SELLS AT A HER NEARBY SHOP AS WELL AS HER OTHER STORE IN BRUSSELS.

OUT OF AFRICA

Bedrooms are spacious with luxurious en-suite bathrooms (opposite). Shades of caramel, coffee, bronze and burnt orange comprise the earthy colour palette here. Bea converts ethnic textiles into curtains by stringing them onto metal curtain rods.

ROUGH LUXE

A low, polished concrete wall divides the bed from the bathroom and doubles as a headboard (above right). The deep terrazzo bathtub, hidden from view from the bedroom side, runs the length of it. Built-in cubbyholes for bathroom products keep useful things to hand and the bather can gaze through a window looking onto the garden as he or she soaks. Bea has accessorized the bathrooms with organic-shaped cork bowls, volcanic lava stones and charcoal-grey towels (above left).

BRIGHT SPOT

A duplex bedroom is decorated with a combination of sober and contrasting primary colours (opposite). The bed is dressed in Society charcoal bedlinen brightened by a collection of Suzani cushions, and the windows are hung with vibrant Indian quilts.

SMALL SHOTS

Joe Colombo's injection-moulded plastic chairs in red and green bring a dash of colour and modernity to a white-painted room and provide a counterpoint to the ethnic textiles (above). A red flokati rug warms the polished concrete floor in the bathroom area. Bea furnishes the rooms with rows of hooks and tall wooden ladders, which function as storage receptacles for towels and clothes.

LIGHT-BULB MOMENT

Throughout the house, bare bulbs hung on twisted black cord supplement the light cast by table and floor lamps. This one is painted with playful stripes that match the colour scheme (left).

Josephine Ekström

Are our homes necessarily a reflection of ourselves? Sometimes, I suspect that they are the opposite: a deflection from an inner maelstrom, a Jungian persona presenting a controlled public face rather than a mirror image. In this case, the serene Josephine Ekström and her home on the coast of Sweden seem to be one living, breathing symbiotic organism; both exude Calm with a capital C.

Scandinavians tend to be discerning about design, approaching interiors with a light hand. An ability to create pragmatic yet beautiful interiors seems to be in their DNA, and there is rarely anything fanciful or ersatz about their taste. Josephine has decorated her home with typical Nordic restraint, but the look she has developed combines classic mid-century Scandinavian furniture with some surprises: darkly glazed Asian ceramics and naive wooden stools, bare light bulbs hung low from twisted black cord, oversized white muslin lanterns juxtaposed with gilded Gustavian mirrors and brutalist concrete-topped tables made by her husband, Rikard.

WHITE ENVELOPE

Josephine's long kitchen divides into
two halves: a galley kitchen fitted with
plain white units and a dining 'room'
at the other end (opposite) where she
has introduced some older pieces;
an 18th-century farmhouse table is
paired with Eames moulded plastic
chairs in black and khaki with splayed
wooden legs (this page), and a black-
and-white Bertoia chair (seen
opposite) used as extra seating.

ATTIC EYRIE

The multitasking attic has areas for relaxing, playing and sleeping. Communal areas are at the centre with bedrooms tucked away under the sloping roof. A dark brown vintage leather sofa bought at auction, a black Bertoia chair and a coffee table made from a wooden pallet are grouped by a window (this page). On a clear day, you can see the sea from here.

MONOMANIA

Josephine has selected a soothing and disciplined palette restricted to greys, blacks, browns and khaki greens (opposite left). Even her young children have become involved in the interior by creating artworks that are casually propped against the wall alongside pictures in gilded frames (opposite right).

The 19th-century house, formerly a general store, on a quiet residential street underwent a meticulous renovation that tackled everything from wiring to surfaces. Existing windows were replaced with some salvaged from a Danish school and chequerboard ceramic tiles, discovered underneath the existing floorboards, were relaid in the entrance hall. The walls were refinished and painted white, and the floorboards treated with a pale oil-based stain. This combination of pale, tactile textures makes a deceptively simple backdrop for Josephine's preferred palette of muted colours: khaki, ochre, charcoal and black. On a mission to restore a historical edge that had been lost over time, they trawled auctions and salvage yards for architectural details that would give the well-proportioned rooms depth and interest.

While the look is spare and considered, the couple have added warmth and texture with clusters of sculptural objects gathered on consoles and coffee tables. Clean, modernist lines are balanced by handmade pieces, the rounded shapes of pottery and weathered wooden ladders and stools. Such artful arrangements might seem too precious for a home to three small children, but Josephine plays with scale, choosing

accessories that are utilitarian and robust: sculptural modern lighting, vintage shop letters and an enormous ball of string, which sits on a low table made from a wooden palette fixed to four castors. There is little pattern, but Josephine has hung bold panels of Deborah Bowness wallpaper and encouraged her children to paint in black poster paint on recycled paper, ensuring a chic collection of naive monochrome art.

Upstairs, Josephine and Rikard opted to remove walls and take the ceiling up to the roof line, exposing the beams and creating an informal attic eyrie with a cosy atmosphere. This space is multipurpose, with zones for work, play and sleep. While the children have bedrooms up here, their parents have placed their bed in a nook, open to the room but tucked under a roof beam on the lower level.

The reinvention of the general store might have changed the floor plan, but the spirit of its past survives. After spending so much time on the project, discovering new and old things, the Ekströms decided to open their own interiors shop. This time the shopping takes place in the kitted-out garage where recycled glass vases, baskets, washed linens, ceramics and sheepskins and diamond-shaped light bulbs line the shelves.

TABLESCAPES

Velvet, leather, concrete and bleached wood combine to give Josephine's ground-floor living room a relaxed and sophisticated rough luxe look (opposite). Josephine's husband Rikard made the coffee table, setting a mighty slab of concrete on a metal base. An unusual table with decorative legs (this page) is sometimes used as a desk, but here its raison d'etre is purely decorative. A plaster nude forms the centrepiece of a still life, surrounded by matt black terracotta jars and vintage wooden bowling balls that were chosen for their scale and texture.

HANG IT ALL

The front entrance hall with its reclaimed chequerboard-tiled floor (below right) opens into a wide stairwell where coats and bags are corralled on a black Ikea clothes rail (opposite). The modernity of the utilitarian rail contrasts with the glossy tiled Swedish stove in the room beyond. In a home with plenty of architectural detail, Josephine's pragmatism both plays down the grander elements and draws attention to them. Throughout the house she has used the most basic lighting: bare bulbs (albeit some shaped like diamonds) hung on twisted black cord, a device that suggests a certain nonchalance. In the attic, Josephine has a reading corner ideal for a design addict, with a wooden bench piled with interiors magazines (below left). On the windowsill she has placed an African mask and a ceramic terracotta pot.

CLEAN, MODERNIST LINES ARE BALANCED BY HANDMADE PIECES, THE ROUNDED SHAPES OF POTTERY AND WEATHERED WOODEN LADDERS AND STOOLS.

COORDINATES

The minimalist wet room (above) is accessorized with grape-grey towels that hang from a heated rail, while extras are stored in large baskets. Amber mosaic towels covering the shower's floor link the bathroom's palette to the rooms beyond.

COLOUR CODE

Instead of a master suite, Josephine has given the attic a floor plan that maximizes communal space for the family. Without a separate bedroom, the grown-ups have taken over a space a few steps down under a beam that's just big enough for a bed and a painted chest of drawers (right). Josephine uses the same linens in subtle shades of grey in every room, giving the whole space a cohesive feel. She keeps pieces of jewellery on an artist's articulated wooden hand (above right).

The uncluttered children's bedrooms are furnished with essentials that also contrive to be decorative: here, a divan bed is tucked into the eaves and a diminutive rail holds a selection of pretty clothes. The primitive rocking horse is both sculptural and useful.

noble salvage

DEFINITION: SCAVENGERS, JUNK JUNKIES, ANTIQUE ADDICTS. REPURPOSING IS NOBLE SALVAGE'S RAISON D'ETRE. BUYING FROM A SHOP IS UNTHINKABLE FOR A NOBLE SALVAGER.

Hilary Robertson

Unless you arrive with buckets of cash, NYC is a tricky place to find a home. After four temporary moves where we sublet and had to live with other people's things, we found our current home, a duplex in a Brooklyn brownstone (a 19th-century vernacular American style of 'row' house). After being set adrift from my ballast of fascinating stuff for too long, I relished the opportunity to decorate and was convinced that this ravishingly corniced, high-ceilinged space was a worthy depository for the contents of the unopened crates that we had shipped over from England.

In the meantime, my husband and I had discovered new sources for our addiction: Hell's Kitchen Flea Market, the antiques shows held at Brimfield, Massachusetts, eBay and the brand-new Brooklyn Flea, which just happened to be on our street. My husband Al had introduced me to the idea that practically anything might form a collection. He foraged for lab glass, Civil War shaving mirrors and sculptor's tools, while I began all over again with studio ceramics, mid-century bookends, signed bronzes, old paintbrushes and artist's palettes. It took us a while to realize that we should acquire something to sit on and a table to eat at, so accustomed had we become to only purchasing the small decorative portable things that we carted from home to home.

We became expert at buying table bases without tops and chairs without legs, and eventually married some of these parts together successfully. Console tables with narrow or demi-lune tops are ideal for smaller rooms and hallways or places where you need a desk but have little room. I like a table that has no other purpose than to be a surface for some pretty still life: a collection, flowers in different-shaped bottles...whatever feels right in the moment. There are two of these in my living room. The white faux bamboo one has a lower shelf that I have loaded with stacks of chalky white chocolate moulds. On the upper surface, I have brought together huge glass jars of shells, coral fans and some pale pink ceramics that contain tiny pieces of coral, crabs and shells. A slim marble slab sitting on a hefty iron industrial base sits on the opposite side of the room, a butch counterpoint to the pink linen chesterfield sofa. It works as a place to put a lamp and as somewhere to play with sculptural objects.

PROP DEPARTMENT

I'm always drawn to anything sculptural. The chalky white chocolate moulds (above left) are very satisfying to arrange, as they can be stacked or balanced in so many ways. The concrete pigeon, a present from my husband, inspired a collection of other inanimate creatures, and our menagerie now includes a fox terrier retrieved from the street, a cat and a rabbit. These grey shelves found at Brimfield Flea (opposite) hold a mass of props. We seem to have created an unintentional ombré effect by placing darker objects on the lower shelves. The graphic black-and-white numbered plank seen to the left of the shelves is a water marker from a canal.

Brownstones have a curious layout; narrow in width but very deep, they usually have rooms that are far from a light source. We decided to paint our ground-floor dining room in blackboard paint, upon which we often draw on or scrawl messages for each other in white chalk. The marble side table is loaded with a collection of Giorgio Morandi-inspired white vessels and above we have grouped our Civil War-era shaving mirrors in the alcove.

As this apartment possesses many useful built-in cupboards, I am able to rotate my accessories on every available surface. One of the most useful items we found at a flea market was a large, grey-painted shelf unit on castors. It found a spot in the dining room on the upper floor and now, laden with multiple collections, serves as my prop department: bird's nests, lab glass, vintage pottery, paintbrushes, balls of string and small paintings are all gathered on the five deep shelves. The still-life possibilities presented on those shelves alone are infinite.

When we first arrived, the whole interior of the brownstone was painted an uninspiring shade of cream that was gradually eradicated. We chose blackboard paint for the dining room. It's a room that gets very little natural light, and so embracing the darkness seemed to be the best approach. Everything else in the room is either white or black, and sometimes we chalk drawings onto the walls. Upstairs in the lofty living room, where the light floods in through tall sash windows, we settled on a highly pigmented greenish-grey tone that somehow magically seems to go with everything, while in our bedroom I picked a sophisticated pinky-taupe shade that teams well with black and white.

This home has developed very slowly. It was our first proper New York home and it grew more comfortable as we did, as, little by little, we adapted to our new environment. The way that we acquired our stuff and the memories of discovery were all part of the slow process of putting down roots. It wouldn't be the same home without all those early flea-market trips. An interior needs to be furnished, yes, but it's the gradual accretion of personal possessions, textures and layers that make it remarkable.

THROUGH A GLASS DARKLY
Along the living room mantelpiece I have lined up arched sections of mirror with a bevelled edge found at the Brooklyn Flea (above and above left). I like the way they reflect architectural detail, and the more 'foxed' the glass is, the better. Dried peony tulips, a violet-shaded dye block and a chunk of rock crystal sit at one end of the marble ledge. The round metal table (opposite) functions as both desk and occasional dining table. The set of painted and gilded chairs came from one of my first visits to New York's 26th Street Garage Flea Market.

I LIKE A TABLE THAT HAS NO OTHER PURPOSE THAN TO BE A
SURFACE FOR SOME PRETTY STILL LIFE: A COLLECTION, FLOWERS
IN DIFFERENT-SHAPED BOTTLES…WHATEVER FEELS RIGHT.

IN THE PINK

The pink linen chesterfield sofa (seen on the previous page) is the only new piece of furniture that I own (it was traded in exchange for styling). However, it seems that I had acquired many pale pink accessories before I owned it (opposite and right), including coral fans, a huge vase of shells, an artist's palette encrusted with shades of pink paint and a sunset painting by a friend, Tobit Roche. The shade introduces some femininity in an otherwise monochrome room.

MIRROR, MIRROR

I keep my jewellery on my bedroom mantelpiece, in a lucite handbag from the 1930s (this page). The line-up here changes daily, but I always keep scent bottles, purses and other accessories visible. The 1940s line drawings of female nudes propped up against the mirror suit the mood of a bedroom, and as they come in a folio of 20, I can change them whenever I like. I rescued my mirrored dressing table (opposite) from a rainy field at Brimfield Flea. I ran towards it, afraid that someone else would get there first. I chose it for its Hollywood glamour, and its diminutive proportions are perfect for this corner of the bedroom.

INTO THE GLOSS

When I moved to New York City, I fell for the furniture that legendary interior designer Dorothy Draper designed in the 1940s and '50s. The glossy black lacquer chest of drawers (opposite), found in a junk shop, has the glamorous Hollywood Regency feel that Draper's look epitomized. The white plywood screen filtering the light was made for the windows at furnishings store West Elm but works perfectly as an alternative to curtains here.

ON A PEDESTAL

The bronze rings by Monica Castiglioni that I wear every day live on this milk-glass cake stand (left) with iconic perfume bottles made in porcelain and a plaster branch, useful for holding rings and bracelets.

Leida Nassir-Pour

If you stroll down George Street, a narrow pedestrian thoroughfare just a few steps from the seafront in Hastings, you would be right to expect the purveyors of sticks of rock, fish and chips and kitsch seaside trinkets that service the day trippers who arrive by the coachload, but Leida Nassir-Pour's thought-provoking and accomplished window displays are bound to stop you in your tracks.

The window of Warp & Weft, Leida's vintage emporium, is likely to showcase a scene plucked from a fairy tale or ballet, or just some romantic vision that's been swimming around in her fertile imagination. A stuffed swan, an 18th-century bridal gown, a pair of antique ice skates or a pristine military dress uniform are the stuff of dreams, which Leida spins into narratives that can't fail to capture the attention of even the most casual passers-by.

After finishing art school, Leida experimented with fine art and photography but eventually came to the conclusion that she wasn't 'good enough' (by her own exacting standards) at either discipline. What she was good at, she decided, was identifying the well-made and the beautiful; when choosing anything from a leather belt to a poem, she had insuperable confidence in her own taste. While living and working in Brighton, she would rise early and dash to the flea market, then immediately sell her finds on to friends and the shopkeepers she was working for at the time. It took a few years of working as waitress, shop assistant and fashion stylist before she realized that choosing was her vocation, and committed to creating her own retail world.

ON THE LEDGE
Leida is a disciplined collector. Never straying from her preferred neutral palette, her shop Warp & Weft has a recognizable signature look. She has a penchant for cleverly cut and detailed vintage clothes, spools of thread, unusual scissors (opposite) and balls of string, which she displays both at home and in her shop on mannequins and mobile storage units (this page) made especially for her from reclaimed wood.

There is something undeniably 'costume drama' about the vintage items that Leida is attracted to: fragile antique wedding dresses for contemporary Miss Havishams, sturdy country tweed jackets for Lady Chatterley's Lovers, trench coats for Quiet Americans; shiny black silk top hats and tails, collar studs, glossy riding boots, duffel coats; superb examples all, which are integrated with Leida's own contemporary collection of clothes that she designs and manufactures herself. Like many skilled merchandisers, Leida can't help but apply her vision to her home as well, where clothes (all in earth tones) too interesting to be hidden away in wardrobes are hung neatly from bespoke racks made from reclaimed wood, shown off by vintage shop mannequins, layered into neatly styled piles in baskets or suspended from rows of hooks.

Five years ago, with a limited budget, Leida and her partner found this corner building, built circa 1828, once a public house and later an antiques shop. Transforming the space has been a long and painstaking process; Leida has a very particular vision and is not one to compromise, but she has the knack of spotting potential everywhere. After stripping the house back to the bone, she salvaged and reused materials wherever she could: the original pub floor was relaid in the garden, salvaged stainless-steel worksurfaces were re-cut to fit her kitchen and the legs of the same surface were recycled from a fishing boat's mast.

When it came to furnishing her home, Leida first had to let go of a cache of pieces that weren't the right scale for the low-ceilinged rooms. However, all those years of buying and selling have trained her to be detached and, much as she nurtures her treasures, she is also able to let them go. Although this doesn't seem to apply to her collection of taxidermy

FUR AND FEATHERS

Leida can't resist taxidermy, skulls and feathers; pheasants, crows, finches and horned beasts congregate on tables and shelves (opposite). She hopes that their presence adds a dream-like quality to her home. In fact, her interior and sartorial style has a Dickensian flavour, with many Victorian and Edwardian items and a washed-out palette of greys, blacks and earthy browns (above right). Grain sacks are used as upholstery for chairs, white monogrammed wedding sheets have been repurposed as curtains and empty frames appreciated for their patina are propped against a wall in the living room (above left).

animals, of which she speaks with particular fondness. She 'animates' her zoo of feathered and furred friends by moving them from room to room, convinced that being surrounded by curious objects evokes certain states, even influences her own dreams and, she hopes, those of her overnight visitors.

Leida's playfulness, and her knack for creating backstories for her possessions, ensures that spending time in both her home and her shop is rather like travelling to a sepia-tinged Dickensian world of orphan pickpockets, cross-dressing tomboys and friendly ravens. Ask her how she feels about colour and she will assure you that the right shade of crimson can make her day, but she only very occasionally allows the smallest dose of it to enter her universe, as she is constantly overwhelmed by visual stimuli and needs to keep her head.

Now that Leida's home is more or less finished, she is apt to wander from room to room, object in hand, improving on still lifes, ordering, rearranging and tweaking with the perfectionist's eager and untiring eye for detail.

UNFITTED KITCHEN

Leida's characterful kitchen demonstrates her talent for creative salvage. Instead of traditional units, a long stainless-steel surface works as a countertop and tiered wire baskets are used as storage (opposite). The butler's sink sits on an old sewing-machine base and a new-fangled washing machine is hidden behind the printed grain sack. On the opposite side of the room, pots and pans are hung with S hooks from a leaning ladder (below). A wooden wall cupboard is filled with neat rows of spices decanted into matching jars. Leida favours well-made kitchen products like the goose-feather dusters and other idiosyncratic brushes devoted to particular household tasks (below left). A stainless-steel shelf unit is home to a host of kitchenalia both beautiful and useful, everything from glass cake stands and cloches to a set of antique scales.

LEIDA'S PLAYFULNESS AND A KNACK FOR CREATING BACKSTORIES FOR HER POSSESSIONS ENSURES THAT SPENDING TIME IN BOTH HER HOME AND HER SHOP IS RATHER LIKE TRAVELLING TO A DICKENSIAN SEPIA-TINGED WORLD OF ORPHAN PICKPOCKETS, CROSS-DRESSING TOMBOYS AND FRIENDLY RAVENS.

BEDTIME STORY

Leida dresses her painted bed, which was made from a weaver's loom, in antique French linen sheets, not minding the frayed edges (above). As she shies away from colour, she chooses to fill a bottle with dried alliums that have faded to a more appropriate straw colour. The mahogany lit bateau with its tall, curved end pieces is tucked into a corner by a window (opposite), making it a cosy place to read and dream. The glazed mahogany cabinet is full of second-hand volumes found in flea markets and junk shops. A buttoned French armchair has been re-covered in vintage linen.

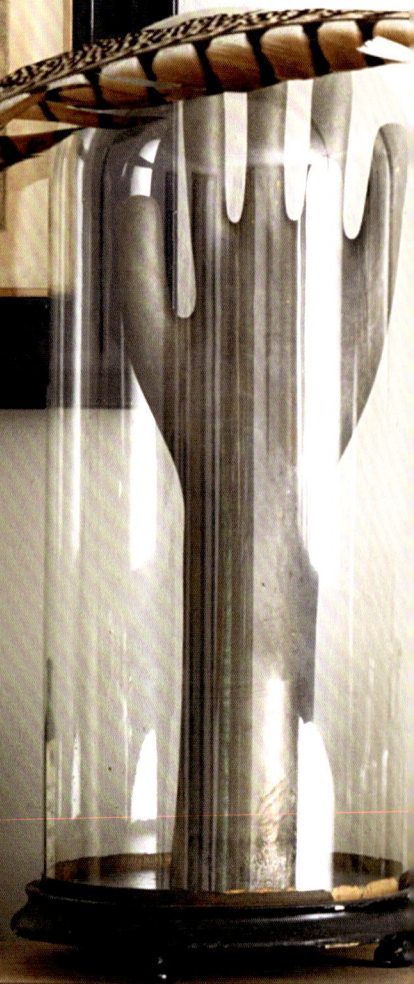

A LONG STORY

Running along a wall next to a bed made from a loom is a rough-textured reclaimed wooden shelf, where antique glass domes (which originally would have covered taxidermy animals) are used to display an early South American vessel and a rubber glove mould. An alligator doctor's bag, a papier mâché head and various apothecary bottles all in shades of brown, ochre and sepia complete the unnerving *mise en scène*.

BATHING RITUAL

A spacious bathroom on the upper floor (this page and opposite) has walls covered in rectangular cream subway tiles and a floor that combines travertine marble brick mosaic tiles with black-and-white tiles used to define the spaces beneath the roll-top bathtub and sink. Leida has made no attempt to hide the copper piping; it is a feature that teams perfectly with the vintage shower head and salvaged taps/faucets (above and opposite). Turkish hammam towels hang from an old wooden ladder as well as a Moroccan metal towel rail, which also has a shelf where the amber pharmacy bottles that Leida collects are displayed (opposite). A dressing mirror on a wooden stand is the best place to apply make-up and lotions (right).

Jocie Sinauer

Jocelyn Sinauer was born in the 20th century, but her home, if not her heart, is planted firmly in the several hundred years that preceded her. As the owner/proprietor of the Red Chair, a captivating shop on antiques row in Hudson, New York, she has surrounded herself with the 17th-, 18th- and 19th-century furnishings, lighting and linens that make her tick. So convincing is Sinauer's gift for merchandising that it could tempt a modernist to turn back; her talent might compel even the most avowed cosmopolite to transform a city apartment into a Swedish farmhouse.

BLUE NOTE
Jocie takes her work home with her,
furnishing the sprawling two-floor
apartment above her store with a
few hard-to-let-go Gustavian pieces:
a painted daybed (opposite), a bureau
(this page) and a 19th-century chaise.
As the rooms are open plan, it made
sense to restrict the palette to shades
of white and blue.

SHADES OF PALE
The upper-floor bedroom is so vast that Jocie has enough room for a tranquil sitting area and a bookshelf devoted to her treasured back catalogue of *The World of Interiors* magazine.

After closing time, Jocie climbs the stairs to the second floor, where she and her husband David Chicane, the chef behind Hudson Food Studio right down the street, have set up house. Living over the store, particularly one filled with fetching furniture, has its advantages. Apart from the convenient work commute, there's the easy access to all those beautiful pieces. And with 370 square metres/4000 square feet over two floors to fill, who could blame the couple for snatching a sofa or cupboard or two for their own? But Jocie, who does most of her shopping in France and Belgium, rarely buys pieces for the store that end up in the house, though she does admit to pilfering the Belgian postal table in her dining room as well as the Swedish cabinet that holds barware and antique glasses there. Not that she hasn't regretted a few sales. There's the 18th-century French glass-fronted cabinet that she would have loved had the apartment had more walls, but she wasn't keen on floating it.

Jocie was smitten with the handsome brick four-storey building, designed by a Dutch boat builder in the 1860s, not only for its upstairs-downstairs ease but also because its generous expanses could handle her predilection for the large furnishings in which she stashes collections she's been amassing for as long as she can remember. As a child growing up in Massachusetts, she and her sisters dug for old bottles behind a friend's early colonial house, then played antiques dealers with each other. When she wasn't unearthing treasures, she collected botanical prints, stamps and coins.

When it comes to Jocie's curatorial eye, it's safe to say genetics plays a role. The daughter of an artist, and the granddaughter of a New York City-based collage artist and decorator, she fondly recalls the visits to Manhattan that involved trawling the streets for tossed-out objects to use in her grandmother's assemblages. Attending auctions the length and breadth of New England was a typical weekend activity for the Sinauer family.

JOCIE WAS SMITTEN WITH THE HANDSOME BRICK FOUR-STOREY BUILDING, ORIGINALLY DESIGNED BY A DUTCH BOAT BUILDER IN THE 1860S.

These days, Jocie is drawn to inlaid boxes, tortoise shells, basalt, old books, snuffboxes and anything nature has to offer, and she arranges them on consoles, armoires and vitrines. An enviable ironstone and creamware collection, displayed along the wall adjacent to the kitchen, is used for everyday meals prepared by her husband, who is as obsessive about beautiful food presentation as his wife is about the table they eat on. His collection of 19th-century copper pots are not just for show; David favours them above all others for cooking.

Jocie has tried countless times to move beyond the texture and patina that has come to define her aesthetic. She loves to tell the story of the beautiful mid-century modern dining-room table and chairs she fell for at a flea market and bought for the store. Minutes after she had arranged them in the shop, she realized that looking at the set drove her mad. She had it removed immediately, and has completely blocked out the name of the designer.

The search for centuries-old pieces will never get old for Jocie, who has recently discovered the beauty – and bounty – of the outer reaches of upstate New York. But her soul remains squarely in Scandinavia; she's currently coveting an 18th-century cabinet with original paint and patina from Sweden, a country where respect for the past is making it harder to find pieces for sale. Jocie Sinauer may just need to move on to a later century yet.

SHIP SHAPE

With so much space, Jocie is able to keep her treasures out on display. Collections here share a nautical theme: a wall (above left) is hung with prints and paintings of boats, while an early Shaker-style side table (opposite) is loaded with coral as well as decorative picture frames. The bureau (above) is stacked with blue marbled paper-bound volumes and the baker's shelves that divide the room from the sitting area are laden with white ironstone pottery jugs, tureens and plates.

BOOKS FURNISH A ROOM

In Jocie's world, books are treated as an essential and decorative accessory, as with the piles of faded, peeling, sepia-tinged antique volumes loaded onto an open bureau in the sitting room (above). However, the simple white shelf unit by the bedroom window (right), with its meticulously arranged stacks of Jocie's favourite interiors magazines, keeps the visual resource easily accessible. The ordered horizontal white spines add another stripe to the mix.

WUNDERKAMMER

The dark khaki-green interior of the 19th-century vitrine (opposite and above right) works as the perfect backdrop for a series of still lifes. Here, Jocie mixes shells, skulls, specimen jars, shapely 18th-century coffee pots, horn candlesticks, classical architectural fragments, snuffboxes, leather-bound books and an oval platter scarred by wear; in fact, all that is pale, interesting and patinated.

FEARFUL SYMMETRY
On the floor above the shop, Jocie's long, narrow dining table, stationed opposite the kitchen counter, is flanked by a group of mismatched chairs. Next to it, a painted vitrine houses glassware, plates, cutlery/flatware and linens. Jocie's symmetrical tablescape balances masculine and feminine elements, with two antique silver candelabra, casual arrangements of peonies in vintage glass jars and a large antler from her collection.

KITCHEN EXHIBITS

The long wooden counter (opposite), which began life in a shop, is used as a room divider, separating the kitchen from the dining area. Less-than-attractive equipment and appliances are concealed behind a curtain of antique linen, while everything else is kept out on display, from silver spoons to the vibrant-orange coffee machine.

SHELVED

Floor-to-ceiling built-in shelves (left) opposite the kitchen house Jocie's extensive collection of ironstone and creamware. Platters and bowls are either stacked in orderly piles or propped up on plate stands so that their shapes and patterns can be appreciated.

LIVING OVER THE STORE HAS ITS ADVANTAGES. APART FROM THE CONVENIENT WORK COMMUTE, THERE'S EASY ACCESS TO ALL THOSE BEAUTIFUL PIECES.

address book

CUSTODIAN

custodian.studio
*Beautiful and functional
traditional brooms made
by hand from US-sourced
materials by Erin Rouse
in Brooklyn.*

JOHN DERIAN

6 East Second Street (between
2nd Avenue and the Bowery)
New York, NY 10003
+1 (212) 677 3917
johnderian.com
*Fine linens, textiles, furniture,
art and accessories.*

DWELL STUDIOS

77 Wooster Street
New York, NY 10012
+1 (646) 442 6000
dwellstudio.com
*Mid-century modern style and
vintage furniture, lighting
and accessories.*

MICHELE VARIAN

400 Atlantic Avenue
Brooklyn, NY 11217
+1 (212) 343 0033
michelevarian.com
*Independent retail at its
best – furniture, tableware,
accessories, lighting,
wallpapers and fabrics.*

THE NEW YORK TIMES STORE

nytstore.com
*Rare and collectible items,
from vintage posters, maps
and newspapers to coins,
models and flags.*

OCHRE

96 Grand Street
New York, NY 10013
+1 (212) 414 4332
ochre.net
*The New York showroom of
these purveyors of Euro-chic
contemporary upholstery,
lighting, mirrors and
home accessories.*

OLDE GOOD THINGS

333 West 52nd Street
New York, NY 10019
ogtstore.com
*Fast-changing stock of rare and
unusual architectural antiques.*

PAULA RUBENSTEIN

195 Chrystie Street
New York, NY 10002
+1 (212) 966 8954
paularubenstein.com
*Vintage textiles, Americana and
industrial vintage furniture.*

RED CHAIR ON WARREN

606 Warren Street
Hudson, NY 12534
+1 (518) 828 1158
redchair-antiques.com
*French, Belgian and Swedish
antiques, all temptingly
merchandized by Jocie Sinauer.*

RH

rh.com
*Nationwide furniture chain
specializing in French- and
Belgian-style reproduction
furniture, hardware and
upholstered pieces.*

TERRAIN

shopterrain.com
*Garden-related furniture,
lighting and accessories –
planters, ceramics, vases and
more. Visit the website for
details of their four locations.*

FLEA MARKETS

BRIMFIELD ANTIQUE FLEA MARKETS

35 Palmer Road
Brimfield, MA 01010
For dates and directions, visit
brimfieldantiquefleamarket.com
*Huge antique and flea market
held three times a year.*

CHELSEA FLEA

29 West 25th Street
New York, NY 10010
*Vintage clothing, original art
and antiques, collectibles,
jewellery and furniture. Every
Saturday and Sunday.*

ORIGINAL ROUND TOP ANTIQUES FAIR

475 Texas HWY 237
Carmine, TX 78932
For dates and directions, visit
roundtoptexasantiques.com
*Enormous triannual flea market
packed with an irresistible
array of antiques, art, decor
and more.*

ROSE BOWL FLEA MARKET

Pasadena, California
For dates and directions, visit
rgcshows.com
*Held on the second Sunday
of each month at Rose Bowl
stadium, come rain or shine.
More than 2,500 vendors.*

SOURCES EUROPE

GALERIE KOPEK

Allée 4 Stand 207
Marché Paul Bert Serpette
110 Rue des Rosiers
93400 Saint-Ouen-sur-Seine
*A treasure trove of unusual and
beautiful antiques curated by
Manolo Vosse, from African
masks to medieval European
sculptures. Follow him on
Instagram @galeriekopek.*

HIROMI

22 Rue Milton
75009 Paris
hiromi-objets.com
*Lighting and other objects
in intriguing organic shapes
designed by ceramicist
Johanna de Clisson. Hiromi
means "free-spirited beauty"
in Japanese.*

MERCI PARIS

111 Boulevard Beaumarchais
75003 Paris
merci-merci.com
*Concept store merchandized
with imagination and style.*

business credits

CAMELLAS-LLORET
MAISON D'HOTES
Rue de l'Angle
11290 Montréal
France
T: +33 6 45 73 96 42
E: annie@camellaslloret.com
www.camellaslloret.com
Pages 18; 48–49; 53; 66–79.

CHAMBRES EN VILLE
www.chambresenville.be
Pages 5; 15; 45–47.

JOSEPHINE EKSTRÖM
LILY & OSCAR
Lerbergsvägen 37
262 32 Höganäs
Sweden
T: +46 (0)70 8288371
E: support@lilyoscar.com
www.lilyoscar.com
*Pages 16; 41; 54–55;
154–163.*

STEPHEN JOHNSON
stephendotcom.com
moonmandotcom.com
Pages 25; 92–97.

YVONNE KONÉ
FASHION DESIGNER
info@yvonnekone.com
www.yvonnekone.com
Pages 40 right; 58–65.

Furniture designed by:
RASMUS JUUL
Københavns Møbelsnedker
Showroom
Sturlasgade 14 P
Islands Brygge
Copenhagen
Denmark
T: +45 33 31 30 30
E: info@kbhsnedkeri.dk
www.kbhsnedkeri.dk
Pages 40 right; 58–65.

SYDNEY MAAG DESIGN
95 Lexington Avenue, Suite 2E
New York, NY 10016
USA
T: +1 631 987 8396
E: Sydney@sydneymaag.com
www.sydneymaag.com
Page 35.

BEA MOMBAERS
BEA B&B
Konijnendreef 6
8300 Knokke-Le-Zoute
Belgium
T: +32 (0)50 603 606
E: items@skynet.be
www.bea-bb.com
Pages 38–39; 142–153.

LEIDA NASSIR-POUR
WARP & WEFT
68a George Street
Hastings
East Sussex TN34 3EE.
T: +44 (0)1424 437180
E: wandwstyling@hotmail.com
Facebook: Warp And Weft Styling
Pages 19; 178–189.

ALINA PRECIADO
DAR GITANE
www.dargitane.com
Pages 20–21; 98–99.

HILARY ROBERTSON
Interiors stylist, vintage and
antiques buyer
T: +1 917 971 7081
E: hilaryrobertsona@gmail.com
www.hilaryrobertson.com
and shop:
MRS ROBERTSON @
GABRIELA DE LA VEGA
88 South Portland Avenue
Brooklyn, NY 11217
USA
www.mrsrobertsonstore.com
*Pages endpapers; 1; 4; 8–13;
17; 22–23; 26–27; 32–33;
42–43; 50–51; 56–57;
110–111; 164–177; 208.*

LIZA SHERMAN
LIZA SHERMAN ANTIQUES
37A Bedford Street
New York, NY 10014
USA
T: +1 212 414 2684
www.lizashermanantiques.com
Pages 28–29; 80–91.

JOCIE SINAUER
RED CHAIR ON WARREN
606 Warren Street
Hudson, NY 12534
USA
T: +1 (518) 828-1158
E: antiques@redchair-
antiques.com
www.redchair-antiques.com
Pages 40 left; 52; 190–201.

LINDSEY TAYLOR
GARDEN DESIGN AND FLORAL
STYLING
T: +1 917 287 8723
E: lindseytaylor@mac.com
http://lindseytaylordesign.com
*Pages 2–3; 30–31; 36–37;
122–129.*

VADUM
COPENHAGEN JADE – A/S.
Head Office
Gammel Kongevej 167C
1850 Frederiksberg C
Denmark
E: info@vadum-cph.com
www.vadum-cph.com
Pages 112–121.

picture credits

All photography by Anna Williams, except where stated otherwise.

Endpapers: The home of Hilary Robertson, interiors stylist and vintage and antiques buyer; 1 The home of Hilary Robertson, interiors stylist, vintage and antiques buyer; 2–3 Lindsey Taylor – garden designer, floral stylist and writer; 4 The home of Hilary Robertson interiors stylist and vintage and antiques buyer; 5 www.chambresenville.be in Brussels; 8–13 The home of Hilary Robertson, interiors stylist and vintage and antiques buyer; 15 www.chambresenville.be in Brussels; 16 The home of the designer Josephine Ekström, owner of Lily & Oscar, in Sweden; 17 The home of Hilary Robertson, interiors stylist, vintage and antiques buyer; 18 The B&B Camellas-Lloret, designed and owned by Annie Moore near Carcassonne/photographed by Claire Richardson; 19 The home of Leida Nassir-Pour of Warp & Weft in Hastings, photographed by Claire Richardson; 20–21 The Brooklyn loft of Alina Preciado, owner of lifestyle store Dar Gitane www.dargitane.com; 22–23 The home of Hilary Robertson, interiors stylist, vintage and antiques buyer; 25 The home of Stephen Johnson; 26–27 The home of Hilary Robertson interiors stylist, vintage and antiques buyer; 28–29 The loft/studio of antiques dealer Liza Sherman at 37a Bedford Street, NY 10014 30–31 Lindsey Taylor – garden designer, floral stylist and writer; 32–33 The home of Hilary Robertson, interiors stylist and vintage and antiques buyer; 35 The home of Sydney Maag in New York; 36–37 Lindsey Taylor – garden designer, floral stylist and writer; 38–39 Bea B&B owned by Bea Mombaers in Knokke-Le Zoute, Belgium www.bea-bb.com; 39 right The country home of the van Mitty family; 40 left The home of Jocie Sinauer, owner of Red Chair on Warren in Hudson, New York; 40 right The home of the designer Yvonne Koné in Copenhagen; 41 The home of the designer Josephine Ekström, owner of Lily & Oscar, in Sweden; 42–43 The home of Hilary Robertson, interiors stylist and vintage and antiques buyer; 45– 47 www.chambresenville.be in Brussels; 48–49 The B&B Camellas-Lloret, designed and owned by Annie Moore near Carcassonne, photographed by Claire Richardson; 50–51 The home of Hilary Robertson, interiors stylist and vintage and antiques buyer; 52 The home of Jocie Sinauer, owner of Red Chair on Warren in Hudson, New York; 53 The B&B Camellas-Lloret, designed and owned by Annie Moore near Carcassonne, photographed by Claire Richardson; 54–55 The home of the designer Josephine Ekström, owner of Lily & Oscar, in Sweden; 56–57 The home of Hilary Robertson, interiors stylist and vintage and antiques buyer; 58–65 The home of the designer Yvonne Koné in Copenhagen; 66–79 The B&B Camellas-Lloret, designed and owned by Annie Moore near Carcassonne, photographed by Claire Richardson; 80–91 The loft/studio of antiques dealer Liza Sherman at 37a Bedford Street, NY 10014 92–97 The home of Stephen Johnson; 98–109 The Brooklyn loft of Alina Preciado, owner of lifestyle store Dar Gitane www.dargitane.com; 110–111 The home of Hilary Robertson, interiors stylist and vintage and antiques buyer; 112–121 The summerhouse of the fashion designer Charlotte Vadum in Denmark; 122–129 Lindsey Taylor – garden designer, floral stylist and writer; 130–141 The country home of the van Mitty family; 142–153 Bea B&B owned by Bea Mombaers in Knokke-Le Zoute, Belgium www.bea-bb.com; 154–163 The home of the designer Josephine Ekström, owner of Lily & Oscar, in Sweden; 164–177 The home of Hilary Robertson, interiors stylist and vintage and antiques buyer; 178–189 The home of Leida Nassir-Pour of Warp & Weft in Hastings/photographed by Claire Richardson; 190–201 The home of Jocie Sinauer, owner of Red Chair on Warren in Hudson, New York; 208 The home of Hilary Robertson, interiors stylist and vintage and antiques buyer.

index

Page numbers in italic refer to the illustrations and their captions

acknowledgements

It takes a village! Thank you to Jess for asking me to come up with an idea for a book and everything else, to Cindy for trudging through a snowstorm to meet me in Brooklyn and everything else, to Annabel for her patience, encouragement and general delightfulness, to Megan for her good cheer and for whipping it all into shape so beautifully. And thanks to Leslie, too, for her behind-the-scenes help.

Thank you to my family, Gus and Al, who have had to put up with a shadow of a mother/wife for far too long! Thanks also to my mother, who thought she might see me when I was on the European leg of the shoot but actually just lived with an enormous suitcase and looked after Gus, my son.

Huge thanks to Kathleen Hackett, my friend, colleague, style sister and fantasy shopping conspirator, for writing the best case studies and for helping me think the whole idea through in the first place on the Public Dock at Hosmer Pond, Maine. And thank you to the hugely talented Anna Williams for her gorgeous pictures and for the fun along the way. I'm so glad that we are both hungry at the same time, Anna. Also to Jeff and Johnny Fogg. Thanks too to photographer Claire Richardson for taking such lovely pictures in Carcassonne and Hastings, and for being a wonderful travelling companion.

Thanks to all the location owners for allowing us to shoot their homes and for looking after us so well. And, lastly, thank you Colin Moore, chiropractor extraordinaire, for sorting out my frozen shoulder.